USING WORD PROCESSING EFFECTIVELY

Barbara Outhwaite

D1784008

McGRAW-HILL BOOK COMPANY

London • New York • St Louis • San Francisco • Auckland
Bogotá • Caracas • Hamburg • Lisbon • Madrid • Mexico
Milan • Montreal • New Delhi • Panama • Paris • San Juan
São Paulo • Singapore • Sydney • Tokyo • Toronto

Published by
McGRAW-HILL Book Company Europe
Shoppenhangers Road, Maidenhead, Berkshire, SL6 2QL, England
Telephone 0628 23432
Fax 0628 770224

British Library Cataloguing in Publication Data

Outhwaite, Barbara
  Using Word Processing Effectively
  I. Title
  652.5
  ISBN 0-07-707269-3

Library of Congress Cataloging-in-Publication Data

Outhwaite, Barbara
  Using word processing effectively / Barbara Outhwaite.
    p. cm.
  ISBN 0-07-707269-3 :
  1. Word processing. I. Title.
  Z52.4.O87 1992
  652.5—dc20   92-12940
                                          CIP

Typeset by Oxprint Ltd, Oxford
and printed and bound in Great Britain by M & A Thomson Litho Ltd, Glasgow, Scotland

CONTENTS

INTRODUCTION FOR STUDENTS

There are three sections in the book each starting with a check-list of the topics covered—both word processing functions and details of correct layout. When you reach the end of a section, it may be useful to go back to the checklist to make sure you are happy about each item mentioned.

Make sure that you have covered all exercises marked with **introducing** in one section before moving on to the next.

About word processors

All word processors carry out similar functions. Operators key in words, phrases and sentences directly on to the screen and make alterations until they are happy with the text. They then save the text on to a disk, and print a perfect copy of the finished text. Word processing is a wonderful tool, but it takes a little practice to learn how to make the most of it, and it is worth the time and trouble.

Since alterations can be made so easily on screen, an extremely high level of accuracy is expected, which anyone can achieve with a little time spent proof reading.

Proof reading

With the exception of the first couple of exercises, when students new to word processing may well need time to adjust to a different keyboard, accuracy **must** become a vital part of the work. Whether you are a 'master' of the typewriter keyboard or not, you can make your work look totally professional by reading every piece of text carefully **on screen**—line by line—before printing. If you develop this habit, it will soon become second nature.

Housekeeping

Disks quickly become full as you work through word processing exercises, and this can cause problems when new work is ready to be stored, in the same way as a filing cabinet becomes full of old files and has to be cleared out. It is a good idea to give your documents logical file names so that you can easily establish which files should be saved and which can safely be erased. The sort of names you can give your files depends on the word processing system you are using (some allow longer names than others, some allow letters and numbers, etc). To begin with it may be helpful to keep a note of file names so that you can quickly identify documents.

We call the regular erasing of 'old' files that are no longer required, '**housekeeping**'. There are 'housekeeping' exercises at various stages in the book, to help you keep your disk clear for new work.

The printer

There are many different kinds of printer currently being used by word processing students. You may have a printer all to yourself, attached to your VDU (Visual Display Unit), or more likely you have to share one with several other students. It will be helpful, at some point, to get to know exactly where the paper should be positioned before printing in order to make the best use of it. As the printer is separate from the keyboard and VDU, and a word processor is not a typewriter, it is quite possible for a document to appear to be perfectly positioned on the paper **on screen**, but to be badly positioned when printed, because the sheet of paper was incorrectly positioned before the printing started. The two basic rules are:

- Get to know your printer
- Treat your printer with great respect.

Default values

Every word processor has pre-programmed settings to determine margins, number of lines per page, and whether the right-hand margin is justified or ragged. Many also have pre-set tab stops. These are known as **defaults**, and they will be applied to any document automatically unless you make a deliberate change. Normally, your 'default' settings will be perfectly adequate for many documents, and you will not need to start altering them straight away. Your understanding of them will develop the more you use your word processor.

Pitch

Pitch refers to the number of characters your word processor produces per inch (2.5 cm). This is a 'default' value which will be pre-set for all documents unless you change it. Many word processors produce 10 characters to the inch horizontally (across), and some produce 12. Usually you can get a setting of 15 if you require it.

The 'inch' referred to here is **on paper**; on screen it may be entirely different so it probably won't be much use taking your ruler and trying to measure the characters on the screen.

```
10 characters to the inch looks
like this.
12 characters to the inch looks like
this.
15 characters to the inch looks like this,
```

Pitch also refers to the number of lines there will be (**on paper**) measured vertically (down). Nearly all word processors produce six lines to the inch, but some differ from this.

1

Checklist of skills

The exercises in section 1 are designed to introduce the following skills. At the end of the section you may like to return to the checklist to make sure that you are confident in each of them.

Word processing functions

▶ CREATING A DOCUMENT

▶ ENTERING TEXT (KEYING IN)

▶ CURSOR CONTROL

▶ USE OF RETURN KEY

▶ PRINTING

▶ SAVING A DOCUMENT

▶ RETRIEVING A DOCUMENT

▶ DELETING CHARACTERS/WORDS/ PHRASES/PARAGRAPHS

▶ INSERTING CHARACTERS/WORDS/ PHRASES/PARAGRAPHS

▶ RE-FORMATTING TEXT

▶ SETTING AND ALTERING MARGINS

▶ USE OF JUSTIFIED AND RAGGED RIGHT-HAND MARGINS

▶ USE OF SINGLE AND DOUBLE LINE SPACING

▶ CENTRING

▶ EMBOLDENING

▶ TAB STOPS

▶ MOVING A BLOCK OF TEXT

Use of correct layouts

▶ FULLY-BLOCKED STYLE OF PARAGRAPH

▶ FULLY-BLOCKED HEADINGS

▶ CORRECT USE OF SPACING FOR PUNCTUATION MARKS

▶ INSET/INDENT TEXT

▶ CENTRED HEADINGS

▶ MENUS

▶ TABULAR DISPLAY

▶ LETTER LAYOUT

Introducing

▶ **KEYING IN**

▶ **USE OF CURSOR**

▶ **CARRIAGE RETURN**

▶ **SAVING**

▶ **PRINTING**

▶ **HEADING**

▶ **BLOCKED PARAGRAPH**

▶ **PUNCTUATION**

Exercise 1

Open a document called X1 and key in the following text. Notice the **fully-blocked** style has been used. Don't worry about any mistakes (for the time being). Press **RETURN** twice after the heading, and twice at the end of the first paragraph, but there is no need to use the **RETURN** key at the end of each line, because the word processor will make the line endings for you.

Spend a little time getting used to moving the cursor around the screen.

Save the document and print one copy.

PUNCTUATION   *press RETURN twice to produce one blank line*

Text produced on a word processor should follow certain rules. Always key in one space immediately after commas, colons and semi-colons; two spaces after full stops, question marks and exclamation marks.

one blank line

When the right-hand margin is justified the word processor will adjust the spaces between words in order to make a straight margin. It is still important to key in the correct number of spaces after punctuation marks, and this is a very good habit to develop.

Introducing

Exercise 2

Open a document called X2 and key in the following text. Use the **fully-blocked** style of layout (just the same as in Exercise 1). Read it through very carefully and correct any mistakes. Save the document and print one copy.

PROOF   READING

press RETURN twice to produce one blank line

Proof reading means the detailed checking of documents before printing to spot and correct any mistakes of spelling, punctuation or layout. It is essential that each document is perfectly correct and accurate before it is printed.

one blank line

It is a very simple matter to make corrections when using a word processor, and so there is no excuse for errors to appear in the printed text. Employers expect a high level of accuracy from their word processor operators.

Introducing

▶ RE-LOADING (RECALLING) TEXT

▶ DELETING

▶ RE-FORMATTING

Exercise 3   Editing text

Re-load (or recall) document X1 and make the following alterations.

1   In paragraph 1, delete the word **immediately**.

2   Re-format (tidy up) the text.

3   Read through the text very carefully and correct any errors.

4   Save the text.

5   Print one copy.

Introducing

▶ INSERTING WORDS AND
   SENTENCES

Exercise 4

Re-load document X2 and make the alterations listed below.

1   In paragraph 1, delete the word **documents,** and insert the word **text,** so that it reads **checking of text before.**

2   In paragraph 2, delete the word **very.**

3   In paragraph 2, line 2, delete the word **is,** and insert the phrase **can be,** so that it reads **there can be no.**

4   At the end of paragraph 2, add the sentence **Try to develop the habit of always checking every document line by line before printing.**

5   Re-format (tidy up) the text.

6   Read through the text very carefully and correct any errors.

7   Save the text.

8   Print one copy.

Introducing

▶ RAGGED RIGHT-HAND MARGIN

Exercise 5

Open a document called X5 and key in the following text using a **ragged right-hand margin** (that is, with the justification switched **off**). Use the **fully-blocked** style of layout (just as in Exercise 1). Save the document and print one copy.

```
THE SOMERSET AND DORSET LINE

The Somerset & Dorset Railway Line, constructed in the nineteenth
century, formed a cross-country link between the south coast and the
Midlands.  The initials S & D were variously interpreted as 'Slow and
Dirty' or 'Swift and Delightful'.

In its heyday it carried many holiday trains from the industrial towns
of the Midlands and north, to south coast resorts such as Bournemouth.
Coal from Somerset coalfields and Mendip stone were carried on freight
trains.

The line attracted much attention from enthusiasts in its final years;
it closed in 1966.  Although today some parts of its old routes show
very little evidence of its former existence, the memory is still dear
to railway buffs.
```

Introducing

▶ JUSTIFIED RIGHT-HAND MARGIN

Exercise 6

Open a document called X6 and key in the following text using a **justified right-hand margin** (that is, with the justification switched **on**). Save the document and print one copy.

```
ACCURACY

A word processor can produce printed documents quickly, depending on the
speed of the printer, but the original text will take as long as it
takes the operator to key it in.  Although it makes life easier to be
able to correct mistakes at the touch of a button, an operator will work
quickly and more efficiently if very few initial errors are made.
```

Introducing

▶ **INSET PARAGRAPH**

Exercise 7

Open a document called X7 and key in the following text using **justified** right-hand margin. Inset the second paragraph by 10 characters. Save the document and print one copy.

```
GOOD CONCENTRATION

A word processor can carry out many complex tasks and has great power
and speed; as a result mistakes can be magnified or files lost or
misplaced very rapidly.  Sometimes this can happen too quickly for the
operation to be cancelled.

          COMMON SENSE

          Almost everyone who operates a word processor will make a
          mistake at some time and lose an item of work as a result.
          Experienced operators tend to make a practice of saving each
          file or document before carrying out any further steps, such
          as printing or editing text.
```

Exercise 8

Re-load document X5 and make the following alterations to the text.

1   Re-format the text so that it is **justified**.

2   In paragraph 1, insert the words **which was**, so that it reads **Line, which was constructed**.

3   In paragraph 2, delete the word **many**.

4   In paragraph 2, insert the word **regularly**, so that it reads **were regularly carried**.

5   Re-format (tidy up) the text.

7   Save the text.

8   Print one copy.

Exercise 9

Re-load the document X6 and make the following alterations to the text.

1   Re-format the text so that it has a **ragged** or **unjustified** margin.

2   Add this text as a second paragraph.

```
It may be useful to keep a dictionary handy, or to use an
on-line spelling checker.  Any time the spelling of a word is in
doubt it can be checked.
```

3   Save the text.

4   Print one copy.

Introducing

▶ LAYOUT

▶ DOUBLE LINE SPACING

Exercise 10

Open a document called X10 and key in the following text in **double line spacing**. Use either a ragged or a justified right-hand margin. Save the document and print one copy.

```
BUTTERFLY OR MOTH?


Butterflies and moths form a large group of insects known as the

Lepidoptera, which differ from all other insects in having wings that

are covered with minute, overlapping scales.  The adult mouth is a long

tube.  There are approximately 2,400 species of Lepidoptera living in

Britain, only 58 of which are butterflies; the rest are moths.


All butterflies fly during the day and most are brightly coloured; moths

tend to fly by night and often have dull colouring.  The antennae (or

feelers) of butterflies are slender and always end in a swollen tip,

whereas there is no standard shape for the antennae of moths.
```

Introducing

▶ ALTERING MARGINS

▶ ALTERING LINE SPACING

Exercise 11

Re-load the document X10 and make the following alterations to the text.

1   Set in the text by six characters at the left-hand margin.

2   Re-format the text to single line spacing.

3   In paragraph 1, delete the word **minute**, and insert the word **tiny**, so that it reads **with tiny, overlapping**.

4   In paragraph 2, delete the word **dull,** and insert the word **drab,** so that it reads **have drab colouring**.

5   Save the text.

6   Print one copy.

Introducing

▶ CENTRED HEADING

Exercise 12

Open a document called X12 and key in the following text in single line spacing. Use a ragged right-hand margin. **Centre** the heading. Save the document and print one copy.

```
                        GOING UP

The first recorded occasion on which human beings broke free from their
earthbound condition was on 21 November 1783, when a balloon built by
the brothers Joseph and Etienne Montgolfier took off from the Bois de
Boulogne in Paris and flew for about 25 minutes.

The Montgolfier brothers had been intrigued to see smoke and particles
of ash rushing up the chimney at home.  They began to fill paper bags
with hot air by holding them over the kitchen fire.  Although they did
not actually understand the physics involved, they went on to produce
the first hot air balloon.
```

Introducing

▶ EMBOLDENING

Open a document called X13 and key in the following text in single line spacing. Use a justified right-hand margin. **Embolden** the headings. Save the document and print one copy.

VIDEOTEX

The term videotex (sometimes known as teletex) refers to any computer system in which text (words and sentences) is received and displayed on a TV or monitor screen.   There are 2 main methods of transmitting information: by TV signals or by public telephone.

TELETEXT SYSTEMS

The term teletext (known as CEEFAX on BBC and ORACLE on ITV) refers to a system in which information is broadcast from a TV transmitter.   It is really a one-way communication system as subscribers simply receive information.   It provides news, sports results, prices of items for sale, weather, etc.   Any of this can be changed at source at any time.

VIEWDATA

The term viewdata refers to a system in which information is sent on the public telephone network and then displayed on a TV set or monitor. Prestel is totally separate from the TV teletext systems: the user needs a viewdata set or an adaptor box.

Open a document called X14 and key in the following text. Use a ragged right-hand margin and double line spacing. **Centre** and **embolden** the heading. Save the document and print one copy.

PIONEER FLIGHT

The Wright brothers' first powered flight on 17 December 1903 is generally considered to be the pioneer aeroplane flight. The Wrights were the first in the world to achieve sustained, controllable, powered, heavier-than-air flight.

They were originally bicycle manufacturers, with a reputation for high-standard work. They drew their inspiration from the study of buzzards in flight, and they invented the first research wind-tunnel which enabled them to build the first successful flying machine.

Exercise 15

Re-load the document X12 and make the following alterations to the text.

1   Set in the text by four characters from the left margin.

2   In paragraph 1, delete the word **condition**, and insert the word **state**, so that it reads **earthbound state**.

3   In paragraph 1, delete the word **about**, and insert the word **approximately**, so that it reads **for approximately 25 minutes**.

4   In paragraph 2, delete the word **actually**, so that it reads **did not understand**.

5   Add this text as a third paragraph.

    At first they sent up a balloon carrying a sheep, a duck and a rooster. All landed safely after flying for nearly 2 miles. A new balloon, of approximately 15 m in diameter, was built with a wicker basket for passengers. The Montgolfiers allowed others to try out their invention, and in the event Francois Pilatre de Rozier and Francois Laurent became the first aeronauts.

6   Save the text.

7   Print one copy.

Exercise 16

Re-load the document X13 and make the following alterations to the text.

1   Re-format the text so that it has a **ragged** right-hand margin.

2   **Centre** all the headings.

3   In paragraph 1, delete the phrase **(words and sentences)**, so that it reads **text is received**.

4   In paragraph 2, insert the phrase **and do not reply**, so that it reads **receive information and do not reply**.

5   Save the text.

6   Print one copy.

Exercise 17

Open a document called X17 and key in the following menu. **Centre** each line. Save the document and print one copy.

```
                    French Onion Soup

        Trout with Duck Pate and Orange Stuffing

            Lamb and White Wine Casserole
                  Stuffed Courgettes
                   Garlic Mushrooms

                 Blackcurrant Sorbet

                 Five Fruit Meringue

                  Coffee and Mints
```

Open a document called X18 and key in the following menu. All lines should be centred, and some are **emboldened**. Save the document and print one copy.

ESPLANADE HOTEL

Lunch Menu

14 August
12 - 2 pm

Mint Pea Soup

Salmon Mousse

Tomato and Anchovy Flan
with Green Salad

Cherry Tart with Ice Cream

Coffee will be served in the Hotel Lounge

Introducing

▶ DIFFERING LINE SPACING WITHIN
A DOCUMENT

Open a document called X19 and key in the following text. Use a justified right-hand margin. Use **double line spacing** in the first paragraph, and **single line spacing** for the rest. Save the document and print one copy.

WHITCHURCH LOCAL HISTORY SOCIETY

23 June

For our June trip we are going to visit historic Berkeley Castle in beautiful Gloucestershire. This has been the home of the Berkeley family since the middle of the 12th century. With its imposing gateway, thick high walls and many fortifications, it resembles a castle from a story book.   Inside, however, it is tastefully furnished, with an interesting collection of paintings, tapestry and antique silver.   We feel sure this will prove a very popular trip.

DETAILS:

Anyone wishing to come please contact Bill Saunders or Janet Richardson; guests are very welcome.   Tickets will be sold on a first-come/first-served basis.

The coach will depart from Novers Road at 1.30 pm, and we expect to arrive home again at 6 pm.

Introducing

▶ TABULAR DISPLAY

Exercise 20

Open a document called X20 and key in the following table. Save the document and print one copy.

```
FLOWERS IN THE POPPY FAMILY

Arctic Poppy         Common Poppy
Greater Celandine    Opium Poppy
Prickly Poppy        Rough Poppy
Welsh Poppy          Yellow Horned Poppy
```

Exercise 21

Open a document called X21 and key in the following table. Save the document and print one copy.

```
SOME VEGETARIAN SOURCES OF PROTEIN

Cereals     Haricot Beans

Mushrooms   Nuts

Pulses      Soya Beans

Soya Milk   Tofu
```

Exercise 22

Open a document called X22 and key in the following table. Save the document and print one copy.

```
CHECK YOUR SPELLING!

Some words people frequently misspell:

definite     definitely    embarrassing

fulfil       fulfilling    fulfilment

install      instalment    separate

separation   sincere       sincerely
```

Exercise 23

Re-load the document X19 and make the following alterations to the text.

1   Re-format the text so that it has a **ragged** right-hand margin.

2   Set in by six characters the heading **details** and the two paragraphs that follow it.

3   In paragraph 1, insert the phrase **to be** in the last line, **this will prove to be a very**.

4   In paragraph 2, insert the phrase **whose addresses can be found on the back page of the newsletter;** so that it reads **Janet Richardson, whose addresses can be found on the back page of the newsletter; guests are very welcome**.

5   Embolden the last paragraph.

6   Save the document.

7   Print one copy.

Exercise 24

Open the document called X24 and key in the following table. Save the document and print one copy.

USEFUL REFERENCE BOOKS

Post Office Guide	Telephone Directories	AA and RAC Books
Dictionary	Encyclopedia	Whitaker's Almanack
BR Timetables	Street Directories	Road Maps
Who's Who	Telex Directories	Post Codes

Introducing

Exercise 25

Open a document called X25 and key in the following text. Use either a ragged or a justified right-hand margin. The letter can be set out exactly as given here (notice that there is **no punctuation** in the address or after **Yours sincerely**. Save the document and print one copy.

```
16 May 19--


17b Montague Road
Whitchurch
BRISTOL
BS9 7DN


Dear Janet

I read in the Whitchurch Local History Society Newsletter that the June
outing will be a visit to Berkeley Castle.  What a lovely idea - I last
went there 10 years ago while I was still at school, so I hope that a
return trip will bring back some happy memories!

As my mother would like to come too, I wonder if you would be kind
enough to send me 2 tickets?  There was no mention of price in the
newsletter, so perhaps you could ring me to let me know how much it will
cost.

Looking forward to seeing you at our next meeting.

Yours sincerely


Rachel Woods
```

Introducing

Exercise 26

Part A

Open a document called X26 and key in the following text in double line spacing. Use either a ragged or a justified right-hand margin. **Embolden** the heading and the final paragraph. Save the document and print one copy.

THE TELEPHONE ANSWERING MACHINE

An answering machine makes use of a tape. The incoming call starts up the tape, which plays a pre-recorded message, the caller then has a short time in which to give his or her message. Afterwards the machine switches itself off in readiness for the next call.

The people who use this equipment may be doctors, veterinary surgeons, dentists or one-man businesses. Secretaries may find it useful to concentrate on an important piece of work for a while and let the machine deal with callers, thus saving them from constant interruption.

A boon for busy people everywhere!

Part B

1   Re-load the document called X26 and **move** the final paragraph **A boon for busy people everywhere!**, so that it becomes the first paragraph (that is, so that it is **between** the heading and the paragraph which begins **An answering machine**).

2   Save the revised document.

3   Print one copy.

Open a document called X27 and key in the following text in single line spacing. Use a justified right-hand margin. Save the document and print one copy.

LOOKING AFTER TACK

A well-kept tack room should emit a lovely smell of freshly cleaned leather. All saddlery is expensive these days and so the tack room should be maintained secure from the possibility of theft. It should also be dry and, if possible, warm, to protect the leather from damp.

Tack should be taken to pieces for cleaning. Dirt and sweat should be removed by washing with tepid water. When the leather has dried, saddle soap should be applied; this will help keep the leather supple and preserve the stitching.

A sign that saddlery has not been properly cleaned is a dark, thick coating of soap, grease, mud or grit. Correctly treated leather should have a deep sheen and not a high polish.

Tack should be kept in a dry place, but away from any artificial heat, which will dry out the natural oils. Humidity and temperature can greatly affect leather: in hot weather it can become brittle, while in cold, damp conditions it may absorb water and feel unpleasantly sodden.

Good quality leather, which has been well-looked-after, will not usually break, but may remain strong and supple for years. Stitching, however, may rot, so it is as well to check it regularly.

Metal parts of saddlery, such as bits, stirrup irons and buckles, should be wiped clean and polished with a dry piece of rag. The tongues of buckles should be oiled to facilitate movement.

Re-load document X27 and make the following alterations to the text.

1   In paragraph 1, delete the word **lovely**, and insert the word **pleasant**, so that it reads **a pleasant smell**.

2   In paragraph 4 , delete the word **any**.

3   In paragraph 5, delete the phrase **well-looked-after**, and insert the phrase **well-cared-for**, so that it reads **has been well-cared-for**.

4   Add the following sentence to the paragraph which begins **Good quality leather**.

    Items to be regularly inspected are: straps, buckles, reins, girths and stirrup leathers.

5   Delete the final paragraph.

6   Re-format the text so that the first paragraph is in double line spacing. The rest should be in single line spacing.

7   Re-format the text so that the first paragraph has a ragged right-hand margin. The rest should have a justified right-hand margin.

8   Save the text.

9   Print one copy.

Open a document called X29 and key in the following text in single line spacing. Use a ragged right-hand margin. Save the document and print one copy.

CACTI AND SUCCULENTS

Succulent plants have been very popular since they were first brought into cultivation. Their unusual and exotic appearance always attracts attention.

Cacti can make a strong initial impact because their appearance is so different from that of other plants. Instead of slender leafy stems, cacti often have swollen stems with spines. Some of their appeal springs from their association with the struggle for survival in a hostile environment.

A flowering cactus has a particular charm. The flowers' delicate beauty contrasts with the plants' elemental appearance, and they frequently sport bright colours.

As well as cacti, many other plants have evolved to survive in arid parts of the world and some have an appearance superficially similar, with fleshy stems and no leaves. Some have a rosette shape with fleshy leaves, others have solid moisture-retaining stems and deciduous non-fleshy leaves. Many of them have leaves of delicate pastel colours, or covered with soft hairs which make the plant very touchable.

Exercise 30

Re-load the document X29 and make the following alterations to the text.

1   In paragraph 1, delete the word **very**.

2   In paragraph 2, change the phrase **initial impact** to **first impression**.

3   In paragraph 2, delete the sentence **Instead of slender leafy stems, cacti often have swollen stems with spines**.

4   In the paragraph which begins **As well as**, change the phrase **in arid parts of the world** to **an arid climate**.

5   Insert the following text as a final paragraph.

    Despite their exotic appearance, these plants are not difficult to
    cultivate, in fact they are among the easiest to grow. Given a porous
    compost, good light, moderate watering and a temperature just above
    freezing, the majority will thrive and even flower.

6   Set in the first paragraph by five characters on both sides.

7   Re-format the text so that the first paragraph has a justified right-hand margin. The rest should have a ragged right-hand margin.

8   Re-format the text so that the first paragraph is in double line spacing. The rest should be in single line spacing.

9   Save the document.

10 Print one copy.

Checklist of skills

Before beginning Section 2, you should at least have completed all the exercises marked **Introducing** in Section 1, and be able to carry out all the functions mentioned in the checklist at the beginning of Section 1.

Proof reading is no less important in this section, and you should be in the habit of

carefully checking every document before printing.

Section 2 is designed to introduce the following skills. At the end of the section you may like to return to the checklist to make sure that you are confident of each of them.

Word processing functions

▶ USE OF UNDERSCORE

▶ ERASING DOCUMENTS FROM DISK

▶ INSETTING TEXT FROM LEFT-HAND AND RIGHT-HAND MARGINS

▶ MOVING BLOCKS OF TEXT

▶ BLANK SPACES MEASURED IN INCHES OR CENTIMETRES WITHIN A DOCUMENT

Use of correct layouts

▶ KEYING IN MEASUREMENTS IN TEXT

▶ CORRECTION SIGNS

▶ NUMBERED AND LETTERED ITEMS

▶ NUMBERED AND LETTERED PARAGRAPHS

▶ ROMAN NUMERALS

▶ USE OF SPACED CAPITALS

▶ KEYING IN MONEY IN TEXT

▶ EXPANDING SHORTENED WORDS

▶ CORRECT MEMORANDUM LAYOUT

▶ CORRECT LETTER LAYOUT

▶ INSERTING DATE IN A LETTER AND A MEMORANDUM

Introducing

▶ LAYOUT

▶ UNDERSCORE

▶ KEYING IN MEASUREMENTS

Exercise 1

Open a document called Y1 and key in the following text using single line spacing and a **ragged** right margin (unjustified).

Note that the heading is underlined. Note also that when measurements are keyed in there is a space between the number and the measurement.

Read the text through very carefully and correct any mistakes.

Save the document and print one copy.

<u>Stationery</u>

Every office has a stationery store. It will usually contain paper of various sizes, envelopes, forms, notebooks, pads, pencils, pens and paper clips.

Typing paper is bought in reams, which are 500 sheets each. Paper is generally produced in standard sizes called International Sizes. The 2 most common sizes produced for office use are A4 and A5. A4 measures 210 mm x 297 mm, and A5 measures 148 mm x 210 mm.

Introducing

▶ HOUSEKEEPING—ERASING DOCUMENTS

Housekeeping

Whichever word processing system you are using it is good practice to do some 'Housekeeping' routines at regular intervals, otherwise the disks can become full and may no longer have room for current work.

Housekeeping simply entails erasing from the disk any document (or file) that is no longer required, in order to make room for new documents. It is rather like sorting through a filing cabinet and discarding any papers that are out of date. It will be necessary to save some documents as they will be recalled later on for revision, while others can safely be erased.

At the moment it is safe to erase all documents from Section 1: that is, **erase all documents from X1 to X30**.

Exercise 2

Open a document called Y2 and key in the following text. Use single line spacing and a **ragged** right-hand margin (unjustified). Save the document and print one copy.

Envelopes

There are many different kinds of envelope in use today, although there is a British Standard specification which covers sizes and terminology. There are 2 main styles of envelope: the Banker envelope and the Pocket envelope. The Banker envelope opens on the longer side, for example, in the case of an envelope 4 in x 10 in the opening will be on the 10 in side. The Pocket envelope opens on the shorter side, so that an envelope 4 in x 10 in will open on the 4 in side.

Introducing

▶ CORRECTION SIGNS

Signs to tell you what alterations to make to the text

One advantage of using a word processor is that it is easy to make alterations to text. Below are the symbols that are used to indicate to the word processor operator what changes to make to a document.

Sign	Meaning
[	New paragraph.
⌐⌐⌐	Two paragraphs to be joined.
⋏	Insert letter or word. Word may be just above the insert mark, or in the margin, or there may be a 'balloon' with an arrow.
└⌐⌐┐	Transpose, which means change the order of the words.
↑ ↓	Transpose vertically, which means change the position of two complete lines of text.
− − − − −	Leave (do not erase) the word that is underlined with a dotted line.
(SPELLING)	Word written in capitals at the margin—giving the correct spelling. It is **not** to be keyed in capitals.
l.c.	Change to lower case (small letters)—word(s) or letter(s) to be altered will be underlined. (Do not underline them unless there is a further instruction to do so.)
caps or u.c.	Change to upper case (capital letters)—word(s) or letter(s) to be altered will be underlined.

Exercise 3

Recall document Y1 and make the following alterations to the text. Save the document and print one copy.

Stationery

Every office has a stationery store. It will usually contain paper of
various sizes, envelopes, forms, notebooks, pads, pencils/ pens and ∧ , erasers
paper clips.

usually
Typing paper is/ bought in reams, which are 500 sheets each. Paper is
generally produced in standard sizes called International Sizes. The 2
most common sizes produced for office use are A4 and A5. A4 measures
210 mm x 297 mm, and A5 measures 148 mm x 210 mm. Standard sizes for

machines and products are necessary to aid international trade.

Exercise 4

Recall document Y2 and make the following alterations to the text. Save the document and print one copy.

Envelopes

There are many different kinds of envelope in use today, although
there is a British Standard specification which covers sizes and
terminology. There are 2 main styles of envelope: the Banker envelope
and the Pocket envelope. The Banker envelope opens on the longer side,
for example, in the case of an envelope 4 in x 10 in the opening will
be on the 10 in side. The Pocket envelope opens on the shorter side, so
that an envelope 4 in x 10 in will open on the 4 in side.

RECTANGULAR

The Post Office has a preferred range of sizes which
it recommends for use, as envelopes within this
range can be more easily sorted by electronic
machines. Envelopes within what is called
Post Office Preferred sizes are not larger than
120 mm x 235 mm and no smaller than
90mm x 140 mm. They should be rectangular
in shape and manufactured from paper weighing
at least 62 grammes per square meter.

Open a document called Y5 and key in the following text in **double line spacing**. Use either a ragged or a justified right-hand margin. Save the document and print one copy.

```
THE COLOSSEUM


This is one of the best known monuments of ancient Rome.  Its original

name was the Flavian Amphitheatre and no one knows why it was given the

name 'Colosseum' later, although it is generally thought that it may be

derived from a colossal statue of Nero which stood near to it.  The name

of the architect of this amazing building is also unknown.  In fact, as

with almost all antiquities, we know little more than what we see today.


The building dates from the first century and is a development from

ancient Greek theatres which were semi-circular in shape (half a

circle), while the Roman amphitheatres doubled-up on this to form a full

circle.  The shape of the Colosseum is an ellipsis (an elongated

circle).  In its day it could hold some 50,000 people.
```

Open a document called Y6 and key in the following text using **double line spacing** and a **ragged** right-hand margin. Save the document and print one copy.

BONSAI

Bonsai is the name given to the art of growing miniature trees, perfected by the Japanese. It began as a naturally occurring process in which the influence of climate, exposure or poor soil quality prevent a tree from growing to its full size.

The Japanese combined their great artistic abilities with the forces of nature to produce these delightfully proportioned Bonsai trees. Sometimes a commercially produced 'Bonsai' may be little more than a dwarfed and stunted imitation, but a truly beautiful one is little short of a masterpiece.

Exercise 7

Recall document Y6 and make the following alterations to the text. Change to a **justified** right-hand margin, and retain double line spacing. Save the document and print one copy.

BONSAI

Bonsai is the name given to the art of growing miniature trees, perfected by the Japanese. It began as a natural~~ly~~ ~~occurring~~ process in which the influence of climate, exposure or poor soil quality prevent a tree from growing to its full size.

The Japanese combined their ~~great~~ _considerable_ artistic ~~abilities~~ _talents_ with the forces of nature to produce these delightfully proportioned Bonsai trees.

u.c. ~~Sometimes~~ <u>a</u> commercially produced 'Bonsai' may _sometimes_ be little more than a dwarfed and stunted imitation, but a truly beautiful one is little short of a masterpiece.

Recall document Y5 and make the following alterations to the text. Change to **single line spacing**. Save the document and print one copy.

THE COLOSSEUM

perhaps

This is ~~one of~~ the best known monument$ of ancient Rome.   Its original

underline name was the <u>Flavian Amphitheatre</u> and no one knows why it was given the

underline name '<u>Colosseum</u>' ~~later~~, although it is generally thought that it may be

nearby

derived from a colossal statue of Nero which stood ~~near to it~~.   The name

of the architect of this amazing building is also unknown.   In fact, as

with almost all antiquities, we know little more than what we see today.

inset this paragraph 6 characters from left margin

|| The building dates from the first century and is a development from

|| ancient Greek theatres which were semi-circular in shape (half a

|| circle), while the Roman amphitheatres doubled-up on this to form a full

actually

|| circle.   The shape of the Colosseum is an ellipsis (an elongated

|| circle).   In its day it could hold some 50,000 people.

Introducing

▶ MEMORANDUM

Open a document called Y9 and key in the following memorandum. Use a ragged right-hand margin.

```
MEMORANDUM

From: Nishita Kaur

To: all staff

14 April 19--


OPENING HOURS

To keep pace with the changing demands of our customers, it has been
decided to extend the hours during which the office is open to the
public.  For an experimental period of six months starting from 1 May we
shall be open at the following times:

8.30 am to 6.30 pm Monday to Friday

9 am to 5 pm Saturday

10 am to 2 pm Sunday

Jane Harris has agreed to come and open up Monday to Friday, so that the
new early start need not affect the rest of the staff, who will arrive
at the usual times.  We will, however, need volunteers to be on a rota
for Saturday and Sunday mornings.

Please see James Wilson for details of overtime rates of pay.
```

Open a document called Y10 and key in the following memorandum with a ragged right-hand margin (refer to Exercise 9 as a guide to the layout). Insert today's date. Save the document and print one copy.

MEMORANDUM

From: John Brent

To: Purchase Department

Date:

PURCHASE OF A NEW DESK

Now that I have moved into my new office I would like you to order a desk for me from our usual supplier. The desk should be capable of taking a visual display unit and keyboard, but must be no wider than 80 cm as I have restricted space.

Recall document Y9 and make the following alterations to the memorandum. Change the date to today's. Save the document and print one copy.

MEMORANDUM

From: Nishita Kaur

To: all staff

14 April 19 -- *use today's date*

OPENING HOURS

we have

times ∧

To keep pace with the changing demands of our customers, ~~it has been~~ decided to extend the/~~hours~~ *times* during which the office is open to the public. For an experimental period of six months starting from 1 May we *underline* shall be open at the following times:

inset by 10 characters

8.30 am to 6.30 pm Monday to Friday   u.c.

9 am to 5 pm Saturday u.c.

10 am to 2 pm Sunday u.c.

first thing

Jane Harris has agreed to come and open up/ Monday to Friday, so that the new early start need not affect the rest of the staff, who will arrive at the usual times. We will, however, need volunteers to be on a rota for Saturday and Sunday mornings.   *continue to*

u.c. Please see James Wilson for details of overtime rates of pay.

Introducing

▶ NUMBERED ITEMS

Exercise 12

Open a document called Y12 and key in the following text. Use either a ragged or a justified right-hand margin.

Note that there is one blank line between each numbered item.

There should be **two** spaces between the number and the text that follows it.

Save the document and print one copy.

```
VIOLET FAMILY

Members of the Violet family, listed below, have flowers with 5 petals:

1   Common Dog Violet

2   Field Pansy

3   Heath Dog Violet

4   Marsh Violet

5   Meadow Violet

6   Northern Violet

7   Sweet Violet

8   Wild Pansy

9   Yellow Wood Violet
```

Open a document called Y13 and key in the following text using either a ragged or a justified right-hand margin. (Refer to Exercise 12 as a guide for the layout.) Save the document and print one copy.

MAKING SIMPLE FLOWER ARRANGEMENTS

It is fairly straightforward to make simple and attractive flower arrangements, if you bear in mind these points:

1 Buy flowers in bud

2 Keep the arrangement simple

3 Cut flowers with differing lengths

4 Make sure blooms do not hide each other.

Open a document called Y14 and key in the following memorandum. Use a justified right-hand margin. Insert today's date. **Note** that the section with numbered items is inset by five spaces from the left-hand margin. Save the document and print one copy.

```
MEMORANDUM

To: Janice Woods

From: Susan Morris

Date:

Telephone Numbers

Would you carry out a complete up-date of the 2 telephone numbers books
currently in use in the office, as we are finding that some numbers have
changed.  Our new telephone system has the capacity for storing the most
common numbers, and I would like to discuss the list with you tomorrow
afternoon.

I suggest these are our most common numbers:

     1   Harris, Browne & Shepton plc

     2   Our Manchester branch

     3   British Rail enquiries

     4   Taxi Rank

Perhaps you have some other suggestions.
```

Recall the document Y13 and make the following alterations to the text. Save the document and print one copy.

```
MAKING SIMPLE FLOWER ARRANGEMENTS
                quite
It is fairly straightforward to make simple and attractive flower arrangements,
if you bear in mind these points:    provided that

1   Buy flowers in bud
                         s
2   Keep the arrangement/ simple
                     to
3   Cut flower stems with differing lengths

4   Make sure blooms do not hide each other

5   Aim for a colour theme.
```

Introducing

Exercise 16

Open a document called Y16 and key in the following memorandum. Use a ragged right-hand margin. Insert today's date. **Note** that when paragraphs are numbered there should be two spaces between the number and the text that follows it. Save the document and print one copy.

```
MEMORANDUM

To all employees

From Security Officer

Ref: DY/BJ

Date:

SAFETY AND ACCIDENT PREVENTION

In order to prevent accidents, all staff should follow this code of practice:

1)  Follow instructions when using equipment, and disconnect any electrical
machines when not in use.

2)  There should be no trailing flexes.

3)  Personal belongings should not be allowed to clutter the floor.

4)  When machines fail to function, call a mechanic, do not attempt amateur
repairs.

5)  Do not smoke in the office, store rooms or where there is any risk of fire.

6)  Typists should take care of correcting fluids, as these may present a fire
risk.

7)  Do not stand on swivel chairs to reach high objects.

8)  Read any notices relating to fire regulations.
```

Open a document called Y17 and key in the following text. Use single line spacing and a ragged right-hand margin. Save the document and print one copy.

CHOOSING THE RIGHT SADDLE

When choosing a saddle for your horse, personal taste comes into play of course, but the saddle must fit correctly or the horse's movement may be impaired, leading to problems such as saddle sores.

The frame on which saddles are built is called a tree, and this is the basis of the size and shape of each saddle. It usually comes in 3 widths to fit narrow, medium and wide horses. To accommodate the different heights of riders, the seat of the saddle is also made in different lengths.

Look for these points:

1) Width - saddles that are too narrow will pinch a horse's withers; those that are too wide will move around and cause galling.

2) Length - a short seat may throw a rider's weight into the cantle of the saddle, and one which is too long may set the rider too far forward.

3) Fit - when the rider is mounted there should always be at least 2 fingers' width clearance between the top of the horse's withers and the underside of the pommel.

Recall document Y16 and make the following alterations to the memorandum. Make sure it is dated for today. Save the document and print one copy.

MEMORANDUM

To all employees

From Security Officer

Ref: DY/BJ

Date:

SAFETY AND ACCIDENT PREVENTION

In order to prevent accidents, ~~all~~ *I would like to* staff ~~should~~ follow this code of practice:

1) Follow instructions when using equipment, and disconnect ~~any~~ *all* electrical machines when not in use.

2) There should be no trailing flexes.

3) Personal belongings ~~should~~ *must* not be allowed to clutter the floor.

5 ̶4̶) When machines fail to function, call a mechanic, do not attempt amateur repairs.

6 ̶5̶) Do not smoke in the office, store rooms or where there is any risk of fire.

7 ̶6̶) Typists should take care of correcting fluids, as these may present a fire risk.

8 ̶7̶) Do not stand on swivel chairs to reach high objects / – *use a step-ladder.*

9 ̶8̶) Read any notices relating to fire regulations.

Thank you for your continued co-operation.

4) *Ensure that equipment is placed securely on desks.*

Introducing

▶ TEXT INSET BY MEASUREMENT

Exercise 19

Recall document Y17 and make the following alterations to the text. Save the document and print one copy.

(CHOOSING THE RIGHT SADDLE) *embolden and centre heading*

inset by one inch (2.5 cm) from left margin

When ~~choosing~~ *you choose* a saddle for your horse, personal taste comes into play of course, but the saddle must fit correctly or ~~the~~ *your* horse's movement ~~may~~ *will* be impaired, leading to problems such as saddle sores.

The frame on which saddles are built is called a <u>tree</u>, ~~and this~~ *which* is the basis of the size and shape of each saddle. It usually comes in 3 widths to fit narrow, medium and wide horses. To accommodate the differing heights of riders, the seat of the saddle is also made in differing lengths.

Look for these points: *underline*

u.c. 1) <u>W</u>idth – saddles that are too narrow will pinch a horse's withers, those that are too wide will move around and cause galling.

u.c. 2) <u>Le</u>ngth – a short seat may throw the rider's weight into the cantle of the saddle, and one too long may set the rider too far forward.

u.c. 3) <u>Fi</u>t – when the rider is mounted there should always be at least 2 fingers' width clearance between the top of the horse's withers and the underside of the pommel. *Back problems may follow if the cantle at the back of the saddle presses down onto the horse's spine.*

If a saddle does not fit correctly the horse's performance is likely to be affected, and he may be liable to a variety of ailments that could eventually make him impossible to ride.

Introducing

Exercise 20

Open a document called Y20 and key in the following text. Use single line spacing and a justified right-hand margin. The first paragraph is inset by half an inch (2.5 cm.) on both sides. Save the document and print one copy.

CLOCHES, BOBS, SHINGLES AND BINGLES

> The cloche hat arrived in 1924, and remained the height of fashion until 1930. It was often worn with a brooch in front. The significant thing about it was that in order to wear it you had to cut your hair short. Once it had appeared there was no future for the traditional coiffure (a bun) which had held sway in 1919-20.

Hair became shorter and shorter, and by 1928, when a style known as the 'Eton crop' became popular, and with many girls wearing trousers, it became difficult to tell them apart from boys. In 1925 the magazine PUNCH carried a joke which ran, 'Grow your hair, man, you look like a girl!'

After the bob came a style called the shingle, then a mixture of each called the bingle. Girls whose hair was straight, curled it with tongs heated on very small methylated spirit stoves, or paid out for a Vasco or Marcel 'permanent wave'.

People have tried to explain why women chose the styles of the twenties. During the war of 1914-18 many women had done men's jobs, and some had cut their hair to work in factories or on farms: they could vote at age 30, and become MPs at 21 - but the only one who actually did so (Lady Astor) was American.

In order to keep your disk clear, it would be a good idea to **erase** the following documents, which will not be needed for any future exercises:

Y1, Y2, Y3, Y5, Y9, Y10, Y13, Y16, Y17.

Retain Y14 as it will be recalled later on in this section.

Exercise 21

Recall document Y20 and make the following alterations to the text. Save the document and print one copy.

CLOCHES, BOBS, SHINGLES AND BINGLES

> The cloche hat arrived in 1924, and remained the height of fashion until 1930. It was often worn with a brooch in front. The significant thing about it was that in order to wear it you had to cut your hair short. Once it had appeared there was no future for the traditional coiffure (a bun) which had held sway in 1919-20.

Hair became shorter and shorter, and by 1928, when a style known as the 'Eton crop' became popular, and with many girls wearing trousers, it became difficult to tell them apart from boys. In 1925 the magazine PUNCH carried a joke which ran, 'Grow your hair, man, you look like a girl!'

After the bob came a style called the shingle, then a mixture of each called the bingle. Girls whose hair was straight, curled it with tongs heated on very small methylated spirit stoves, or paid out for a Vasco or Marcel 'permanent wave'.

People have tried to explain why women chose the styles of the twenties. During the war of 1914-18 many women had done men's jobs, and some had cut their hair to work in factories or on farms: they could vote at age 30, and become MPs at 21 - but the only one who actually did so (Lady Astor) was American.

Introducing

▶ MOVING PARAGRAPHS (SEVERAL)

Exercise 22

Open a document called Y22 and key in the following text in single line spacing. Use a ragged right-hand margin. Save the document and print one copy.

```
MATERIALS FOR CALLIGRAPHY

Calligraphy is the name given to the art of beautiful writing, a skill that
enables you to develop your own personal style at the same time as practising a
rigorous discipline.  Some of the basic materials required are listed below.

A range of PENS is useful, including ball-points, fibre-tips and special
calligraphy pens.  Pencils are needed for ruling-up the page.

PAPER is essential, of course.

Choose a DRAWING BOARD approximately 60 cm x 45 cm in size.

A 30 cm wooden or metal RULER will be useful, as well as a transparent plastic
one.

Good quality fountain pen INKS will be adequate for practising, but special
CHINESE INKS are better for finished work.

A good-sized TABLE will provide plenty of room to work.
```

Exercise 23

Recall document Y22 and make the following alterations to the text. Save the document and print one copy.

```
MATERIALS FOR CALLIGRAPHY

Calligraphy is the name given to the art of beautiful writing, a skill that
enables you to develop your own personal style at the same time as practising a
rigorous discipline.  Some of the basic materials required are listed below.

A range of PENS is useful, including ball-points, fibre-tips and special
calligraphy pens.  Pencils are needed for ruling-up the page.

PAPER is essential, of course.

Choose a DRAWING BOARD approximately 60 cm x 45 cm in size.

A 30 cm wooden or metal RULER will be useful, as well as a transparent plastic
one.

Good quality fountain pen INKS will be adequate for practising, but special
CHINESE INKS are better for finished work.

A good-sized TABLE will provide plenty of room to work.
```

Open a document called Y24 and key in the following memorandum. (Refer to Exercise 16 as a guide to the layout.) Use single line spacing and a ragged right-hand margin. Save the document and print one copy.

MEMORANDUM

To Receptionist

From Security Officer

Date

SECURITY IN THE RECEPTION AREA

Our firm has many visitors in the course of the day, a large proportion of whom are strangers. In order to ensure the security of our staff and property, these are the rules that will apply to the Reception Area.

1) Strangers must not be allowed to walk around the premises unaccompanied. Please call the department concerned, and politely ask the visitor to wait for an escort.

2) The firm's employees all carry WORKS PASSES, which will be checked by the commissionaire.

3) Please notify me at once if you receive a telephone message that a bomb has been left in the building – even if you suspect it's a hoax. The police will have to be informed and the building cleared.

4) Cameras or large bags should not be carried by visitors past the Reception Area, but should be left for collection later: large bags could be used to smuggle out goods, and cameras might be used to photograph confidential work! Perhaps you could try to keep an eye on these items till their owners return.

Thank you for your co-operation, and please contact me if you have any problems at all.

Recall document Y24 and make the following alterations to the memorandum. Use today's date. Save the document and print one copy.

MEMORANDUM

To Receptionist

From Security Officer

Date

SECURITY IN THE RECEPTION AREA

Our ~~firm~~ *complex* has many visitors ~~in~~ *during* the course of the day, a large proportion of whom are strangers. In order to ensure the security of our staff and property, these are the rules that will apply to the Reception Area. l.c.

2 1) Strangers must not be allowed to walk around the premises unaccompanied. *underline*
Please call the department concerned, and politely ask the visitor to wait for an escort.

1 2) The firm's employees all carry WORKS PASSES, which will be checked by the commissionaire. *Please check that your own is up to date.*

4 3) Please notify me ~~at once~~ *immediately* if you receive a telephone message that a bomb has been left in the building – even if you suspect it's a hoax. The police will have to be informed and the building cleared.

3 4) Cameras or large bags should not be carried by visitors past the Reception *l.c.*
l.c. Area, but should be left for collection later: large bags could be used to smuggle out goods, and cameras might be used to photograph confidential work! Perhaps you could try to keep an eye on these items till their owners return.

Thank you for your co-operation, and please contact me if you have any problems at all.

Open a document called Y26 and key in the following text using a ragged right-hand margin. Use double line spacing, except for the numbered paragraphs. Use single line spacing for the numbered paragraphs, and inset them by one inch (2.5 cm.) from both margins. Save the document and print one copy.

FEEDING YOUR PET

All animals take in food which their bodies convert to energy. Energy is measured in calories. An animal needs to take in a certain amount of energy to do the things it needs to do.

Animals also need food to build bones and muscles, teeth and claws, etc. A healthy diet should consist of a mixture of the basic food groups.

When planning your pet's diet, remember that he needs the same basic food groups as you.

> 1 Carbohydrates: found in bread, biscuits, potatoes, vegetables and fruit.
>
> 2 Protein: found in meat, eggs, milk and some vegetables especially pulses and peas.
>
> 3 Vitamins and trace elements: found in many foods, although they can be given as a food supplement.
>
> 4 Hydrocarbons: fats and oils.

You can obtain more information from the MANUAL OF NUTRITION, issued by the Ministry of Agriculture, Fisheries and Food, but if you use your common sense, and remain sensitive to your pet's changing needs (for example, more food in winter than in summer), he should thrive.

Open a document called Y27 and key in the following text. Use a justified right-hand margin. The first paragraph should be in double line spacing, and inset by half an inch from both margins. Save the document and print one copy.

FEEDING YOUR PARROT

> There are many different kinds of parrots, and they all need a
>
> different type of diet, but they should all be given branches of
>
> fruit trees or willows to chew on, partly to prevent them chewing
>
> up their surroundings, and partly because they consume some of the
>
> bark which may well provide them with necessary nourishment.

Parrots differ both in size and requirements, but here is a basic list of the foods they should be given:

Fruit	Potatoes
Green vegetables	Rolled oats
Hemp seed	Root vegetables
Meal worms	Rice (cooked)
Nuts of any kind	Spray millet
Peanuts	Sunflower seed
Plain canary seed	Wild plants

Stale bread or cake soaked in honey and water, honey and milk or fruit juice
Wholemeal digestive biscuit crumbled with boiled egg

All these birds should have a regular supply of mineral grit and fresh clean water.

Recall document Y26 and make the following alterations to the text. Change to single line spacing throughout. Save the document and print one copy.

FEEDING YOUR PET ← *centre and embolden heading*

All animals take in food which their bodies convert to energy/ ~~Energy~~ *which* is

measured in calories. An animal needs to take in a certain amount of energy to

do the things ~~it~~ *he* needs to do.

He ~~Animals~~ also needs food to build bones and muscles, teeth and claws, etc. A

healthy diet should consist of a mixture of the basic food groups.

When planning your pet's diet, remember that he needs the same basic food

groups as you.

2 ~~1~~ Carbohydrates: found in bread, biscuits, potatoes, vegetables and fruit.

1 ~~2~~ Protein: found in meat, eggs, milk and some vegetables especially pulses and peas.

4 ~~3~~ Vitamins and trace elements: found in many foods, although they can be given as a food supplement.

3 ~~4~~ Hydrocarbons: fats and oils.

You can obtain more information from the MANUAL OF NUTRITION, issued by the

Ministry of Agriculture, Fisheries and Food, but if you use your common sense,

and remain sensitive to your pet's changing needs (for example, more food in

winter than in summer), he should thrive.

5 Water: may be drunk, or supplied in a variety of foods.

Recall document Y27 and make the following alterations to the text. Change to a ragged right-hand margin. Save the document and print one copy.

FEEDING YOUR PARROT

↕ 2 line spaces here

change
to single
line
spacing

There are many different kinds of parrots, and they all need a

different type of diet, but they ~~should~~ all ~~be given~~ *require* branches of

(fruit trees) or (willows) to chew on, partly to prevent them chewing

up their surroundings, and partly because they consume some of the

bark which ~~may well~~ *is thought to* provide them with necessary nourishment.

Parrots differ both in size and requirements, but here is a <u>basic list</u> of the
foods they should be given: *underline*

Fruit	Potatoes
Green vegetables	Rolled oats
Hemp seed	Root vegetables
Meal worms	Rice (cooked)
Nuts of any kind	Spray millet
Peanuts	Sunflower seed
Plain canary seed	Wild plants

Stale bread or cake soaked in honey and water, honey and milk or fruit juice
Wholemeal digestive biscuit crumbled with boiled egg

↕ 2 line spaces here

u.c. <u>All these birds should have a regular supply of mineral grit and fresh clean</u>
<u>water</u>.

Introducing

▶ SPACED CAPITALS

▶ MONEY

Exercise 30

Open a document called Y30 and key in the following text. Use a ragged right-hand margin. **Note** that the heading is centred and in **spaced capitals**, the title is emboldened, the first paragraph is in double line spacing, and the final paragraph is inset one inch (2.5 cm.) from both margins and is in single line spacing. Save the document and print one copy.

S T A I N W Y C H   A M A T E U R   D R A M A   S O C I E T Y

Present

THE MATCHSTICK

by

Brenda Wright

This is a powerful play set in nineteenth century Manchester. Although it

carries a serious, thought-provoking theme, it builds up to a very dramatic

climax and provides excellent family entertainment. We are sure you will enjoy

it, and go home thinking about the issues raised.

> The venue is LONDONVALE ROAD COMMUNITY CENTRE, and
> performances will take place on:
>
> Thursday 18 October
> Friday 19 October
> Saturday 20 October
>
> Tickets, priced at £3 per adult and £1.50 per child
> under 14, are available in advance from members of the
> society, or at the door.

Open a document called Y31 and key in the following text. Save the document and print one copy.

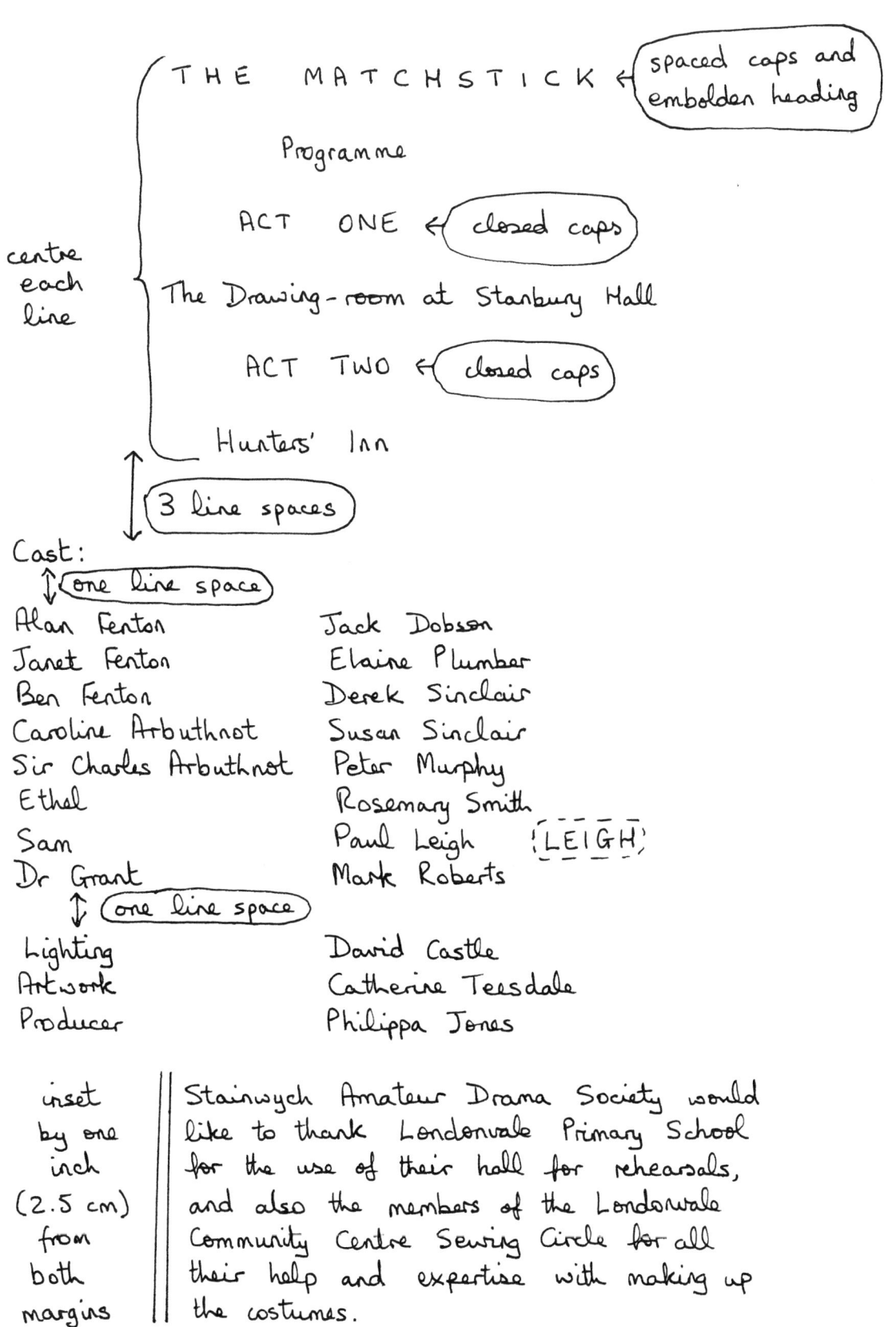

THE MATCHSTICK ← spaced caps and embolden heading

Programme

ACT ONE ← closed caps

The Drawing-room at Stanbury Hall

ACT TWO ← closed caps

Hunters' Inn

centre each line

3 line spaces

Cast:

one line space

Alan Fenton   Jack Dobson
Janet Fenton   Elaine Plumber
Ben Fenton   Derek Sinclair
Caroline Arbuthnot   Susan Sinclair
Sir Charles Arbuthnot Peter Murphy
Ethel   Rosemary Smith
Sam   Paul Leigh   [LEIGH]
Dr Grant   Mark Roberts

one line space

Lighting   David Castle
Artwork   Catherine Teesdale
Producer   Philippa Jones

inset by one inch (2.5 cm) from both margins

Stainwych Amateur Drama Society would like to thank Londonvale Primary School for the use of their hall for rehearsals, and also the members of the Londonvale Community Centre Sewing Circle for all their help and expertise with making up the costumes.

Recall document Y31 and make the following alterations to the text. Save the document and print one copy.

T H E   M A T C H S T I C K

Programme

ACT ONE
The Drawing-room at Stanbury Hall

ACT TWO
Hunters' Inn

(in order of appearance)

Cast:

Alan Fenton	Jack Dobson
Janet Fenton	Elaine Plumber
Ben Fenton	Derek Sinclair
Caroline Arbuthnot	Susan Sinclair
Sir Charles Arbuthnot	Peter Murphy
Ethel	Rosemary Smith
Sam	Paul Leigh
Dr Grant	Mark Roberts
Lighting	David Castle
Artwork	Catherine Teesdale
Producer	Philippa Jones

u.c.

change to double line spacing

extend grateful

Stainwych Amateur Drama Society would like to thanks to Londonvale Primary School for the use of their hall for rehearsals, and also the members of the Londonvale to Community Centre Sewing Circle for all their help and expertise with making up the costumes.

Introducing

▶ **ABBREVIATED WORDS**

When people are writing pieces of work by hand that are later going to be keyed into a word processor, they sometimes use **shortened forms** of words to save time. It is expected that the word processor operator will realise that these **short forms** should be printed in full (and correctly spelt). It is very common, for example, to use 'approx' for 'approximately', or 'advert' for 'advertisement', but the shortened forms of the words are not acceptable in professional, printed material.

Below is a list of some of the shortened words to look out for, with the correct form beside them.

accom.	accommodation	mfrs.	manufacturer(s)
a/c (s).	account(s)	misc.	miscellaneous
ack.	acknowledge	mtg.	meeting
advert (s).	advertisement(s)	opp (s).	opportunity(ies)
appt (s).	appointment(s)	rec (s).	receipt(s)
approx.	approximately	rec.	receive
Ave.	Avenue	recd.	received
bel.	believe	recom.	recommend
bus.	business	ref (s).	reference(s)
cat (s).	catalogue(s)	rfd.	referred
cd.	could	resp.	responsible
cttee	committee	sec (s).	secretary(ies)
co (s).	company(ies)	sep.	separate
comp (s).	competition(s)	sig.	signature(s)
Cres.	Crescent	suff.	sufficient
def.	definite(ly)	temp.	temporary
dif.	different(ce)	tho.	though
Dr.	Drive	Rd.	Road
dr.	dear	sh.	shall
exp (s).	expense(s) or experience(s)	shd.	should
ffy.	faithfully	sin.	sincerely
gov (s).	government(s)	wh.	which
gntee (s).	guarantee(s)	w.	with
immed.	immediate(ly)	yr.	your or year
incon.	inconvenient(ce)		

Days of the week should also be printed in their full forms: Monday, not Mon., Tuesday, not Tues., and so on. The same applies to the months of the year: January, not Jan., February, not Feb., and so on.

Common abbreviations such as etc, eg, can still be used.

Open a document called Y33 and key in the following text using single line spacing and a justified right-hand margin.

Note that the **shortened words** (such as wh., yr., wd. and so on) should be printed **in full**, and that the full stops which follow them are not punctuation but are a way of drawing the word processor operator's attention to the fact that the word has been shortened. The abbreviation 'etc' should be retained.

Save the document and print one copy.

ELTON RIDING CLUB

INFORMATION SHEET 4

We have listed below some activities wh. you may enjoy now that you have acquired yr. new pony. These are only brief outlines, and a further Information Sheet is available covering each one in more detail – just ask at the office for whichever one you wd. like.

HACKING

This is simply having a pleasant ride in the countryside – an enjoyable way of keeping yr. pony fit! Slow work is essential for hardening up muscles.

GYMKHANAS

These are comps. wh. give new riders the opportunity to have a great deal of fun and put their newly acquired skills into practice: stopping, turning, backing, etc.

SHOW JUMPING

The larger shows are run according to British Show Jumping Association rules, and to enter any of their classes you need to be a BSJA member. But there are plenty of shows at all dif. levels – look out for shows put on by yr. local church cttee. or sports club.

SHOWING

Showing classes are comps. for horses and ponies of exceptionally good appearance – so don't bother unless yr. pony is a real good looker! You cd. enter Breed classes if yr. pony is pure bred, you would need to be able to produce its 'papers' – the evidence of its breeding, however. If you have a nicely behaved animal, you cd. show off its quiet behaviour in Working classes – best get to know yr. pony first, tho.!

Open a document called Y34 and key in the following text. Use single line spacing, except for the first paragraph, and a ragged right-hand margin.

Note that any shortened words should be printed in full, and that when the abbreviation e is used, the word 'and' should be keyed in. The abbreviation 'etc' should be retained.

Save the document and print one copy.

THE BLACKBIRD

double line spacing

Blackbirds are very common e welcome visitors to our parks and gardens. They are most numerous in winter when they migrate to the British Isles from the continent.

How to recognise these birds

They are quite large. The male is all black in colouring w. a yellow bill and eye-ring, dark eyes e legs. The female has dark brown upper parts, pale throat e dark rust underparts mottled w. dark brown; she has a dark bill, yellow eye-ring, e dark eyes e legs. The babies are similar to the female in appearance, but paler and more mottled.

Their song

They make a low 'tchook', or a repetitive 'tchink-tchink' if alarmed. Their song is beautiful e well-known, particularly noisy at dusk.

Their food

They eat worms, grubs, caterpillars, etc from the ground, soft fruit from bushes, e search among dead leaves for seeds and insects.

Nesting

They build a cup made from leaves, grass and mud, in bushes or outhouses. Eggs are laid between late March e July, and are light blue-green in colour w. a reddish-brown sprinkling of speckles.

Recall document Y33 and make the following alterations to the text. Save the document and print one copy.

ELTON RIDING CLUB *(heading in spaced caps and emboldered)*

INFORMATION SHEET 4

inset by one inch (2.5 cm) from both margins

We have listed below some activities which you ~~may~~ *can* enjoy now that you have acquired your new pony. These are only brief outlines, and a further *of cou[rse]* Information Sheet is available covering each one in more detail – just ask at the office for whichever one you would like.

HACKING

This is simply having a pleasant ride in the countryside – an enjoyable way of keeping your pony fit! Slow work is essential for hardening up muscles.

GYMKHANAS

These are competitions which give new riders the opportunity to have a great deal of fun and put their newly acquired skills into practice: stopping, turning, backing, etc.

SHOW JUMPING

The larger shows are run according to British Show Jumping Association rules, and to enter any of their classes you ~~need~~ to be a BSJA member. But there are *have* plenty of shows at all different levels – look out for shows put on by your local church committee or sports club.

SHOWING

Showing classes are competitions for horses and ponies of exceptionally good appearance – so don't bother unless your pony is a real good looker! You could enter Breed classes if your pony is pure bred, *but* you would need to be able to produce its 'papers' – the evidence of its breeding ~~, however~~. If you have a nicely behaved animal, you could show off its quiet behaviour in Working classes – best get to know your pony first, though!

An hour or 2 a day over a period of 4 to 6 weeks will get most ponies fit.

Recall document Y34 and make the following alterations to the text. Change to a justified right-hand margin. Save the document and print one copy.

THE BLACKBIRD ← spaced caps and underline

Blackbirds are (very) common and ⌄welcome visitors to our parks and gardens.

They are most numerous in winter when they migrate to the British Isles from

the continent.

How to recognise these birds

They are quite large. The male is all black ~~in colouring~~ with a yellow bill and eye-ring, dark eyes and legs. The female has dark brown upper parts, pale throat and dark rust underparts mottled with dark brown; she has a dark bill, yellow eye-ring, and dark eyes and legs. The babies are similar to the female in appearance, but paler and more mottled.

Their song

They make a low 'tchook', or a repetitive 'tchink-tchink' ~~if~~ when alarmed. Their song is [beautiful] and [well-known,] particularly noisy at dusk. ∧ and

Their food

They eat worms, grubs, caterpillars, etc from the ground, soft fruit from bushes, and search among dead leaves for seeds and insects.

Nesting

They build a cup made from leaves, grass and mud, in bushes or outhouses. Eggs are laid between late March and July, and are light blue-green in colour with a reddish-brown ~~sprinkling of~~ speckles.

Open a document called Y37 and key in the following text using single line spacing and a justified right-hand margin. **Note** that in 'lettered' items there should be two spaces between the letter and the text that follows it, and there should be one blank line between each item.

ELTON   RIDING   CLUB

INFORMATION SHEET 8: SHOWING CLASSES

If - and only if - your horse or pony has <u>outstanding</u> physical make-up these classes may be worth considering. Some marks are given for performance, but appearance is the deciding factor. It is rare to find a good show pony - don't be afraid to ask members of our staff for their opinion - but if yours is a nice-looking and well-behaved animal there is certainly nothing to stop you using these shows to gain valuable experience.

Before a show, groom your pony well, see that the tack is clean, and dress correctly yourself.

In the ring with other ponies, try to:

(a) Keep a reasonable distance from the pony in front.

(b) Ride in a wide circle.

(c) Have a short display worked out in advance.

(d) Be polite at all times.

(e) Remember that the judge's decision is final.

Any of the staff here at the Riding Club will be happy to give advice and help, but remember, the important thing is to ENJOY YOURSELF!

Open a document called Y38 and key in the following text. Use either a ragged or a justified right-hand margin, and single line spacing (except for the 'lettered' items). Save the document and print one copy.

VACANCIES   SHEET ← spaced caps

The co. is currently able to offer the following vacancies:

inset by
one inch   Company Secretary
(2.5 cm)   Marketing Manager

Applications shd. be sent to the Personnel Department by the last Fri. of the month.

JOB   DESCRIPTIONS ← closed caps

The Co. Sec. holds a key position in this organisation, and the successful candidate will be resp. for the following:

inset by   a) Keeping a Register of Shareholders
one inch   b) Organising mtgs.
(2.5 cm)   c) Making statutory returns
             d) Administration of the organisation.

The Marketing Manager carries the resp. of marketing our goods & services. The newly appointed Marketing Manager will control these areas:

                 a) Market Research
                 b) Credit Control
inset by   c) Publicity
one inch   d) After-sales Service
(2.5 cm)   e) Export Sales
                 f) Packing
                 g) Transport

The departments concerned will be able to furnish more details, if required.

Exercise 39

Recall document Y37 and make the following alterations to the text. Save the document and print one copy.

ELTON RIDING CLUB

INFORMATION SHEET 8: SHOWING CLASSES

If – and only if – your horse or pony has <u>outstanding</u> physical make-up these classes may be worth considering. _Some marks are given for performance, but appearance is the deciding factor. [It is / ~~rare~~ very rare to find a good show pony – don't be afraid to ask members of our staff for their opinion – but if yours is a nice-looking and well-behaved animal there is certainly nothing to stop you using these shows to gain valuable experience.

Before a show, groom your pony well, / *plait his mane,* see that the tack is clean, and dress correctly yourself.

In the ring with other ponies, try to:

inset by one inch (2.5 cm)

(a)   Keep a reasonable distance from the pony in front.

(b)   Ride in a wide circle.

(~~d~~) d Have a short display worked out in advance.

(~~d~~) e Be polite at all times.

(~~d~~) f Remember that the judge's decision is final.

Any of the staff here at the Riding Club will be happy to give advice and help, but remember, the important thing is to ENJOY YOURSELF!

However good looking any pony may be, he will not be awarded prizes unless he behaves quietly and jumps without any bother. For this reason your pony may sometimes be in with a chance over a more expensive show animal.

(c) Listen carefully to the judge's instructions.

Recall document Y14 and make the following alterations to the text. Change to a ragged right-hand margin. Remember to use today's date. Save the document and print one copy.

```
MEMORANDUM

To: Janice Woods

From: Susan Morris

Date:

Telephone Numbers

Would you carry out a complete up-date of the 2 telephone numbers books
currently in use in the office, as we are finding that some numbers have
changed.  Our new telephone system has the capacity for storing the most
common numbers, and I would like to discuss the list with you tomorrow
afternoon.

I suggest these are our most common numbers:

    1  Harris, Browne & Shepton plc

    23 Our Manchester branch

    34 British Rail enquiries

    45 Taxi Rank

Perhaps you have some other suggestions.
```

2 Fisher & Sons plc

The head of the A/cs. Department has suggested to me that we cd. arrange for 2 new extensions, one for his office and one for the Print Room. I would be grateful if you wd. look into the possibility, e find out the costs involved. Whilst I understand how incon. it must be for Print Room staff to be without a telephone, I also want to be certain that any new exp. is really necy. before we proceed.

(NECESSARY)

Let me have yr. thoughts.

In order to keep your disk clear, it would be a good idea to **erase** the following documents, which will not be needed for any future exercises:

Y14, Y20, Y21, Y22, Y24, Y26, Y27, Y30, Y31, Y33, Y34, Y37, Y38.

In fact, you can start working on the next exercises (Exercise 41 onwards) without any of the previous exercises still stored on disk, if you wish.

Exercise 41

Open a document called Y41 and key in the following text using a ragged right-hand margin.

Note that when Roman numerals are used to number items, there should be two spaces between the **widest** of the numbers (in this case, iii) and the text that follows it, then the other items should be 'lined-up' accordingly.

Save the document and print one copy.

PLAYING BADMINTON

SOME COMMON STROKING FAULTS

There are a number of common faults which can be corrected with a little thought and practice:

i   Lack of wrist

ii   Poor position when hitting the shuttlecock

iii Not keeping your eye on the shuttlecock

iv   Incorrect racket angle

Introducing

▶ <u>LETTER WITH TABULAR DISPLAY</u>

Exercise 42

Open a document called Y42 and key in the following letter using a ragged right-hand margin. Save the document and print one copy.

14 May 19--

Mr H Calthorpe
Manager
Western Bank plc
Weston
READING
RG5 3MV

Dear Mr Calthorpe

REQUEST FOR A LOAN

I aim to set up in business as a retailer selling perfumes and beauty
products, and I shall need some financial help in the form of a loan to
cover my initial expenses.

There is a small shop available - number 12 Cheltenham Road - which would
be ideal for my purposes. It is part of a rank of shops which includes a
supermarket, a bank, a baker's shop, a florist and a newsagent, and all of
these shops would attract customers whilst there is no direct competition,
not even a chemist, nearby.

Below is a breakdown of what I expect to make:

	£
Net profit before paying myself a salary	18,000
ADD	
Sales value of goods used by me	1,000
LESS	
What I could earn elsewhere	15,000
Realistic profit	<u>3,000</u>

Perhaps I could arrange to come into the bank and talk to you about my
finances.

I look forward to hearing from you.

Yours sincerely

Janet Palmer

Open a document called Y43 and key in the following letter using a ragged right-hand margin. Remember that abbreviated words should be printed in full (the abbreviation 'eg' should be retained). Save the document and print one copy.

18 May 19--

Miss J Palmer
125 Stephens Cres.
Weston
READING RG12 4NV

Dear Miss Palmer

Bank Loan caps

Thank you for your letter of 14 May. It is our usual practice to meet the customer before considering the possibility of offering a loan, & so my sec. has made an appt. for you on 29 May at 2 pm, which will give us the opp. to have an informal discussion.

I wd. be grateful if you wd. let us know whether this will be convenient.

As you will understand, we have a duty to make certain that any money the bank lends will be secure, but we also wish to protect you from the risk of falling into debt. The important question we will need to answer is: is yr. bus. going to be profitable? We shd. be able to answer this on the basis of some relatively simple figures.

It would be helpful if you cd. provide the following details:

i   A brief outline of yr. personal details - like a CV (retain abbreviation)
ii   Details of yr. personal means, eg property
iii Comprehensive details of the shop concerned (12 Cheltenham Rd.)
iv   Any market research you have carried out
v   An estimate of gross profits per month from turnover
vi   A cash flow forecast
vii The amount of finance required and any security you can offer.

In the meantime, if we can help with advice, please contact us.

Yrs. sin.

H Calthorpe
Manager

Open a document called Y44 and key in the following letter using either a ragged or a justified right-hand margin. Save the document and print one copy.

Date as postmark

Leave 8 clear line spaces
for the address

Dear Customer

BEAUTY MARK - the NEW boutique in Cheltenham Road

There is an exciting new shop about to open in Cheltenham Road. Come and sample all our beauty products and browse amongst the perfumes!

The famous actress Stevie Bingham will attend our opening on Saturday 1 September at 2 pm, and there will be a FREE draw at 2.30 pm when the first 5 names pulled from the basket will each win a presentation pack of high quality beauty products.

For the rest of the afternoon, and all day on Monday 2 September our exclusive range of Country Scene perfumes will be on special offer:

	USUAL PRICE	SPECIAL OFFER PRICE
Spring Fever	£6.50	£3.25
Summer Madness	£7.20	£3.60
Autumn Mist	£5.80	£2.90
Winter Glow	£7.10	£3.55

In addition there will be many other offers, and FREE samples for our customers during our first week of trading.

We look forward to seeing you!

Yours sincerely

Janet Palmer
Manageress

Recall document Y44 and make the following alterations to the letter. Save the document and print one copy.

~~Date as postmark~~ *use today's date*

Ms Y Johnson
43a Westminster Dr.
Walton Park
READING   RG12 3NP

Dear ~~Customer~~ *Ms Johnson*

BEAUTY MARK - the NEW boutique in Cheltenham Road

You are invited to

inset by one inch (2.5 cm) from both margins

There is an exciting new shop about to open in Cheltenham Road. *Come and* l.c. sample all our beauty products and browse amongst the perfumes!

TV star

The famous /~~actress~~ Stevie Bingham will attend our opening on Saturday u.c. 1 September at 2 pm, and there will be a FREE draw at 2.30 pm when the first 5 names pulled from the basket will each win a presentation pack of

finest ~~high~~ quality beauty products/

For the rest of the afternoon, and all day on Monday 2 September our exclusive range of Country Scene perfumes will be on special offer:

	USUAL PRICE	SPECIAL OFFER PRICE
Spring Fever	£6.50	£3.25
Summer Madness	£7.20	£3.60
Autumn Mist	£5.80	£2.90
Winter Glow	£7.10	£3.55

inset by one inch (2.5 cm) from both margins

In addition there will be many other offers, and FREE samples for our customers during our first week of trading.

We look forward to seeing you!

Yours sincerely

Janet Palmer
Manageress

, worth £50. At 3pm champagne will be served with a light buffet.

Recall document Y41 and make the following alterations to the text. Save the document and print one copy.

PLAYING BADMINTON :

SOME COMMON STROKING FAULTS

There are a number of common faults which can be corrected with a little thought and practice:

i   Lack of wrist

ii   Poor position when hitting the shuttlecock

iii Not keeping your eye on the shuttlecock

iv Incorrect racket angle.

↕ 2 clear line spaces here

The following hints may help.

LACK OF WRIST – *Correction*: loosen yr. grip on the racket until you actually hit the shuttlecock.

POOR POSITION – *Correction*: bend yr. knees a little when preparing to smash; & remain flexible at the waist.

INCORRECT RACKET ANGLE – *Correction*: think about your grip and ~~footwork~~.

NOT KEEPING YOUR EYE ON THE SHUTTLECOCK – *Correction*: watch the shuttlecock all the time never taking yr. eye away from it for an instant.

Unless you are a 'natural' sportsman or sportswoman, it will be to your advantage to practise several of the strokes of this game until you are proficient. No one expects to 'pick up' a musical instrument without plenty of effort & suff. hours going over difficult pieces of music. Why should it be different with a sport?

Open a document called Y47 and key in the following letter using either a ragged or a justified right-hand margin. Save the document and print one copy.

```
Ref: UP67897


(Use today's date)

CONFIDENTIAL

Miss B E Williams
67 Sydenham Road
Grace Park
SOUTHAMPTON   SO8 6LB

Dear Miss Williams

PERSONAL PENSION PLAN
                                        retain abbreviation
                                               ↓
The incentive payment has now been received from the DSS in respect of your
Personal Pension Plan.

I have pleasure in enclosing a unit statement showing the allocation to
units of the incentive.

Should you require any further information concerning your Personal Pension
or other investment or life assurance matters, please contact your
financial advisor or Shaftsbury & County representative.

Yours sincerely
SHAFTSBURY & COUNTY ASSURANCE SOCIETY LIMITED



G T Howard
Administration Manager


Enc
```

Open a document called Y48 and key in the following letter using either a ragged or a justified right-hand margin. Remember that abbreviations should be printed in full (the abbreviation 'WC' should be retained); refer to page 55 for a list of abbreviations. Exercise 47 can be used as a guide to layout.

Save the document and print one copy.

Ref: TN/SG

(Use today's date)

BY HAND

Mr J Watkins
Flat 4
17 Woodland Gdns.
GRIMSBY
South Humberside   DN12 7KG

Dear Mr Watkins

12 CHARLTON DRIVE

I bel. this property wd. suit your requirements well, and strongly recom. that you make an appt. to view it as soon as possible, as it is certain to attract considerable interest.

I enclose details, e look forward to hearing from you. (I have not yet recd. a photograph, but when I do I sh. pass it on to you immed.)

Thank you for your interest in the above mentioned property. [12 Charlton Dr. is a delightful cottage with very pretty gardens, pleasantly situated in a quiet village location, yet only approx. 4 miles from the motorway and 12 miles from the city centre. The accom. comprises a cosy living-room, kitchen-diner, 2 good-sized bedrooms and a modern bathroom w. sep. WC, and is very well presented e ready for immed. occupation. The roof has recently been re-tiled, and it has damp e timber grtees. still in force.

Yrs. sin.
HAROLD BLAKE & PARTNERS

Jennifer Pope

Enc

Introducing

▶ BLANK SPACES IN THE TEXT
(VERTICAL MEASUREMENT)

Exercise 49

Open a document called Y49 and key in the following text using a ragged right-hand margin.

Note that, in order to measure accurately the spaces required for the blank 'box' you will need to know the **pitch** your word processor works in, that is, how many characters there are to the inch (or 2.5 cm.) horizontally (across), and how many lines to the inch (or 2.5 cm.) vertically (up and down).

Save the document and print one copy.

```
HAROLD BLAKE & PARTNERS ESTATE AGENTS
```

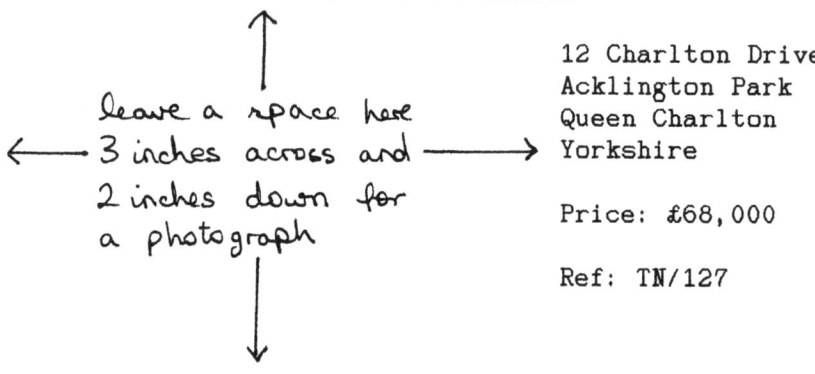

```
                                        12 Charlton Drive
                                        Acklington Park
                                        Queen Charlton
                                        Yorkshire

                                        Price: £68,000

                                        Ref: TN/127
```

```
A superb period cottage tucked away in a quiet, almost tranquil, position
in the delightful village of Acklington!

Immaculately presented accommodation, with pretty gardens and fully
modernised interior, make this a property not to be missed!

The accommodation comprises:

SITTING ROOM * FITTED KITCHEN * 2 GOOD-SIZED BEDROOMS * LUXURY BATHROOM *
LOVELY GARDENS * PARKING * QUIET LOCATION *

VIEWING: By appointment with the agent Harold Blake & Partners.
Telephone: 465783

OPENING HOURS: Monday to Friday      -  9 am - 6 pm*
               Saturday             -  9 am - 5 pm
               Sunday               - 10 am - 4 pm

* After hours appointments by prior arrangement.
```

Exercise 50

Open a document called Y50 and key in the following text using a ragged right-hand margin.
Save the document and print one copy.

SHAFTSBURY & COUNTY ASSURANCE SOCIETY LIMITED

(embolden heading)

ANNUAL UNIT ALLOCATION STATEMENT (spaced caps / 2 spaces between words)

(2 clear line spaces here)

PLAN NUMBER   UP67897

PLAN TYPE   MONEY SAVER

POLICY HOLDER

(retain abbreviation)

| Fund | Type of Unit | No. of Units | Bid Value |
| With Profit | Accumulation | 253.67 | £ 355.14 |

Please read this statement in conjunction w. the Policy Conditions
to find out if a deduction applies on early surrender.

Exercise 51

Open a document called Y51 and key in the following letter using a justified right-hand margin.
Save the document and print one copy.

(Use today's date)

Mr J Watkins
Flat 4
17 Woodland Gdns.
GRIMSBY
South Humberside DN12 7KG

Dear Mr W————

I have today recd. details from Stephen Bates & Partner of yr.
proposed purchase of the property known as 12 Charlton Dr. [I have
put in hand a local search & have written to the Vendors'
solicitors requesting a draft contract.

Yrs. sin.

Brian Fletcher

Recall document Y50 and make the following alterations and additions to the text. Save the document and print one copy.

SHAFTSBURY & COUNTY ASSURANCE SOCIETY LIMITED ← *centre heading*

one clear line space here

Miss B E Williams   22 July 19--
67 Sydenham Road
Grace Park
SOUTHAMPTON SO8 6LB

one clear line space here

A N N U A L   U N I T   A L L O C A T I O N   S T A T E M E N T ← *embolden*

3 clear line spaces here

one clear line space between each line

PLAN NUMBER   UP67897

PLAN TYPE   MONEY SAVER

POLICY HOLDER   BRENDA E WILLIAMS

single line spacing

This statement shows the number of Life Fund units allocated to this plan as at 22 July 19--, together with the bid value on that date.

one clear line space here

one clear line space between each line

Fund	Type of Unit	No. of Units	Bid Value	u.c.
With Profit	Accumulation	253.67	£355.14	
	Total Bid Value		£355.14	

single line spacing and inset by one inch (2.5 cm.) from both margins

This statement takes into account premiums paid up to and including that due on 5 July 19--.

Please read this statement in conjunction with the Policy Conditions to find out if a deduction applies on early surrender.

Recall document Y51 and make the following alterations and additions to the letter. Change to a ragged right-hand margin. Save the document and print one copy.

Ref: JBP/RH

(Use today's date)

Mr J Watkins
Flat 4
17 Woodland Gardens
GRIMSBY
South Humberside   DN12 7KG

Dear Mr Watkins

12 CHARLTON DRIVE

I have today received details from ~~Stephen Bates~~ Harold Blake & Partner of your proposed purchase of the property ~~known as 12 Charlton Drive.~~ above as

I have put in hand a local search and have written to the Vendors' solicitors requesting a draft contract.

Yours sincerely
JONATNAN COX e CO SOLICITORS

~~Brian Fletcher~~ Jane B Porter

I have also recd. a telephone call from Mrs Jackson's solicitors informing me that she has put her sig. on her part of the contract e that they are ready to exchange contracts as soon as I have given them the relevant information concerning the management of the block.

This is the information requested on the questionnaire wh. I sent to you recently. I understand that Mrs J—— is looking for a completion date about the middle of next month.

Open a document called Y54 and key in the following table. Save the document and print one copy.

```
                    COLUMN ONE              COLUMN TWO
                    Annual returns          Annual returns
                    in local currencies     in sterling

% per annum         Average 1975-84         1975-84*

Australia           18.1                    21
Canada              15.4                    20
France              19.4                    19
Germany             12.5                    16**
Hong Kong           26.6                    30
Japan               14.8                    25
Netherlands         22.2                    27
Singapore           17.9                    27
Switzerland         10.0                    18
USA                 14.8                    23
United Kingdom      31.7                    32

 *  Figures have been rounded up
 ** Excluding German tax credit
```

Open a document called Y55 and key in the following memorandum using either a ragged or a justified right-hand margin. Insert today's date. (Refer to Exercise 9 as a guide to layout.) Save the document and print one copy.

MEMORANDUM

From Pete

To Geoff

Can you make sure that a rec. was sent to Brian Daul to ack. his payment for the advert. wh. we published in last month's journal.

I spoke to Mr Daul on the telephone this morning, e I bel. they have not ~~that received~~ any communication at all from us this yr.: I explained that since Alison left we have had a temp. sec. in the office, who is still finding her feet, but I would like this matter cleared up immed.

Would you also check that all local gov. circulars have been correctly filed, as there seems to be a pile of misc. papers lying in a basket on Jan's desk at the moment. [I have noticed that our cat. is not completely up to date, with some mfrs. ~~wrongly~~ incorrectly listed. This should be sorted out this week, if possible.

Recall document Y54 and key in the following letter, making sure that the table is inserted in the correct place. Use a ragged right-hand margin. **Note** that there is an enclosure mentioned in the final paragraph, so **Enc** should be keyed in at the end. Save the document and print one copy.

Today's date

Ms R Patel
198 Thatcher's Rd.
TAUNTON
TA3 1LJ

Dr. Ms P——

INTERNATIONAL EQUITIES

Thank you for your letter in wh. you ask our advice on investments. I recom. that you consider spreading yr. money into some foreign investments. Below is a table to show you how currency affects the return on international equities:

Yrs. sin.
HOLD & BAGSHOTT INVESTMENT ADVISORS

Kate Simpson
Investment Consultant

With an international trust you have 2 sources of growth — the share holdings & the currency.

My sec., Gill, will telephone you within the next few days to arrange an appt. for me to come & visit you to talk this matter over. In the meantime I am enclosing our investment pack for u.c. you to read.

3

Checklist of skills

Before beginning Section 3, you should have completed all the exercises marked **Introducing** in Section 1, **all** the exercises in Section 2, and you should be able to carry out all the functions mentioned in the checklists at the beginning of Section 1 and Section 2.

Proof reading is still a very important part of the work if you are to be a competent word

processor operator, and you should be in the habit of carefully checking every document before printing.

Section 3 is designed to introduce the following skills. At the end of the section you may like to return to the checklist to make sure that you are confident of each of them.

Word processing functions

▶ AUTOMATIC PAGE NUMBERING

▶ HEADERS

▶ FOOTERS

Use of correct layouts

▶ STANDARDISING NUMBERS IN TEXT

▶ STANDARDISING PARAGRAPH STYLES

▶ STANDARDISING HEADINGS

▶ USE OF INDENTED PARAGRAPHS

▶ ALPHABETICAL ORDER

Housekeeping

In order to keep your disk clear, it would be a good idea to **erase** the following documents, which will not be needed for any future exercises:

Y41, Y42, Y43, Y44, Y47, Y48, Y49, Y50, Y51, Y54, Y55.

In fact, you can start working on Section 3 without any of the previous exercises stored on disk, if you wish.

Introducing

▶ STANDARDISING NUMBERS IN
TEXT

Exercise 1

Open a document called Z1 and key in the following text using a justified right-hand margin.

Note that when there are several numbers in a text they should be 'standardised' to avoid a random mixture of figures and words. A simple rule to follow is:

- All numbers should be keyed in as digits
- **Except** — the number **one** (which should always be a word), and
  - — when the number **begins the sentence**.

The passage below contains various numbers; notice how they are presented.

Save the document and print one copy.

<pre>
                            JUMPING

PREPARATION

For jumping, your stirrup leathers need to be 2 or 3 holes shorter than for
hacking. The reason for this is that you have to raise your body out of
the saddle while jumping and shorter leathers make it easier to do so.

As an introduction to jumping, walk the pony over a pole lying on the
ground. Use a pole about 4 inches thick which the pony will be able to see
without difficulty and which will not be broken if he treads on it.

Approaching the pole from either side, trot over it once or twice and then
repeat the exercise at the canter.

Now raise the pole about 6 inches and do the same thing.

CAVALLETTI

This is a good type of jump for the beginner. The poles are fixed to cross
pieces at each end so that the height of the pole alters when the ends are
rotated. Six inches from the ground is the lowest height, 18 inches the
highest. The cavalletti trains the horse to look where he is going, pick
his feet up and approach obstacles calmly.

A line of cavalletti will normally consist of 6 or more poles all set at
the same height and positioned in a straight line at about 4 foot
intervals. A single jump can be made by placing one pole from the
cavalletti on top of another, or by standing 2 poles side by side. The
overall height should be about 18 inches and the width about 2 feet.
</pre>

Open a document called Z2 and key in the following text using a justified right-hand margin.

Note that the numbers in the text should be 'standardised' (refer to Exercise 1 as a guide).

Note that the American spelling for some words has been used, and should be **retained**: **offense**, **defense** and **center**.

Save the document and print one copy.

INTRODUCING AMERICAN FOOTBALL (spaced caps & embolden)

Teams and Officials

American Football is played by two teams, each having 11 players on the field at 1 time. 1 team is always the attacking team (the offense) and the other the defending team (the defense). The offense is the team who have possession of the ball.

Many professional clubs have squads of forty-five players. Each squad consists of 3 teams: an offensive team, a defensive team and a special team. They will also have some reserves.

7 officials control the game, all of whom carry a yellow weighted duster which they throw to the ground when a foul is spotted. The senior official is the referee who always indicates a call. In the National Football League the referee can be distinguished from his colleagues by his black cap – the others wear white caps.

THE OFFENSE

The eleven players on the offense are made up of a center, 2 guards, two tackles and 2 ends. These players form the offensive line and are then supplemented by a quarterback and running backs.

THE DEFENSE

The defense will usually consist of 1 nose guard, two tackles and linebackers. The remaining players, normally 4, are called the secondary or defensive backs and they may be either safeties or cornerbacks.

Introducing

Exercise 3

Open a document called Z3 and key in the following text using a ragged right-hand margin.

Note that the headings differ in style, but should be keyed in using **one** style. The paragraphs also differ in style, and should be **standardised**.

Save the document and print one copy.

USING HERBS

Herbs will add an exotic taste to any dish. Herbs such as chives, parsley and mint tend to be used a great deal, yet there are many more available, fresh or dried, to give our cooking an individual flavour. Some less well-known ones are described below.

Basil

Originally this came from India and Iran, but is now grown in many European countries, especially those with warm climates. It has long slim leaves and tender stems. It has a mild yet pungent flavour and tastes good with tomato.

Coriander

Originally this came from Asia and Southern Europe, but it is now used in many countries. The leaves are flat and delicately coloured. It is best used fresh rather than dried.

MARJORAM

This came from Western Asia and the Mediterranean but now grows extensively in France. It is associated with love and romance. Its leaves are grey-green. It tastes good with lamb, salads, green beans and chicken.

Garlic

Garlic is a member of the onion family. It came originally from Asia, but is now grown worldwide. It grows in bulbs and is associated with good health. Its strong flavour is loved or hated.

Rosemary

This originated in Mediterranean countries but is now grown profusely all over Europe. It is associated with legends and is mentioned in 'Hamlet'. The leaves are grey-green and are like thick and curved needles. It goes well with pork and lamb.

THYME

Originally from Southern Europe, thyme still grows profusely in its native lands. The leaves are greenish-brown and small. It tastes good with tomato, fish and white sauce dishes.

Introducing

▶ PAGE NUMBERING

▶ ALPHABETICAL ORDER

Exercise 4

Recall document Z3 and make the following alterations and additions to the text. **Rearrange** the paragraphs into **alphabetical order** (according to the name of each herb) and insert the additional paragraphs accordingly. **Note** that all headings and paragraphs should be **standardised**.

The revised document will now go into two pages: **number** each page **top centre**.

Save the document and print one copy.

Bay Leaves
The bay leaf originated from the Mediterranean ~~countries~~ ~~area~~ and is now also grown in Mexico. The leaves are shiny and deep green & may be as long as 3 inches (7.5 cm). It is used in pickles, marinades & meat stews.

Dill
Originally from Southern Europe & the Middle East, dill is now grown in all temperate countries. In appearance it is a little like fern. It goes well with cucumber & potato salad.

Tarragon

('BEARNAISE') Tarragon grew originally in Siberia and Asia, & moved to Southern Europe and France during the Middle Ages. The leaves are (deep green) & (slim). It is an essential ingredient of Bearnaise sauce and adds a distinctive flavour to salad dressings, fish stock, Tartare sauce, vinegar & omelettes.
CARAWAY SEEDS

(SAUERKRAUT) These are native to Europe, especially Holland. The leaves are short & curvy, light brown in colour, and very hard and pointed. They are used to flavour the liqueur called Kummel, & go well in rye bread, sauerkraut, Hungarian Goulash and Old English seed cake.
Sage
Sage is native to Europe, & was used by the ancient
u.c. greeks and romans. It has soft green leaves, & tastes good with pork & bacon.
MIXED HERBS
This is a blend of (dried) or (fresh) herbs & can be used in many
l.c. dishes. It usually contains basil, oregano, Marjoram & thyme but may also be made from parsley, chives and chervil.

Open a document called Z5 and key in the following text. **Note** that layout should be **standardised**.

Number pages at bottom centre.

Save the document and print one copy.

LOCATION OF A RETAIL OUTLET (centre)

Where sh. I site my shop?

In a large shopping centre the ~~potential~~ possibility of achieving a high turnover may be better, but the rents and bus. rates may be correspondingly high. Generally speaking, it is better to go to the big Shopping l.c. l.c. Centres for high turnovers, but a small, sole trader will be l.c. competing w. the Multiples who have well-known names to attract customers.

/ACCESSIBILITY/

It is generally agreed that accessibility is critical to the success of a shopping centre. This means that it shd. be close to main roads, car parks, bus routes, and in a places where many people are likely to pass by. [If you are considering opening a shop, look at such things as the size of the local population, especially in terms of the kind of people likely to use yr. shop.)

l.c. Visit the Planning Department resp. for the area – there may be plans in the pipeline to restrict parking, to encourage or for discourage people thinking of settling in the area.

The simplest way for a retailer to maximise profits is to maximise turnover, and the most obvious way to do this is to site yr. shop in an easily accessible location such as an established shopping centre. You must analyse and collect all kinds of information, however, before making a decision.

It is as well to make sure that the ~~population~~ size of yr. catchment area will be large enough to support your shop, and if you are considering taking over an existing bus. you will need to go over the a/cs.)

The owner may be selling because he cannot build up his turnover, e this may be because the local population is too small. Alternatively the population may be ~~quite~~ large, but there may be competition from other, similar shops.

THE MARKET L.C.

The 'market' of a shopping centre refers to the total number of people using it and likely to use it. Factors that may influence the 'market' are:

1 Population of the area.

2̶3̶ Distance people are prepared to travel to shop (eg, in the London area people seem ready to travel greater distances to shop than in other parts of the country).

3̶4̶ Car ownership.

4̶5̶ Competition from other Shopping Centres. L.c.

5̶6̶ Communication:

    (a) local newspapers

    (b) local radio

6̶7̶ 'Business' attractions of a shopping centre:

    a department stores with well-known names wh. attract ∧customers ∧many

    b the type of items & services offered for sale

    c the reputation of the larger stores at the centre

    d whether banks are available

    e car parks, bus routes, etc.

2 Class of consumer

The attraction of the shopping centre will be based on:

1) The (quality) and (number) of the shop units

2) Compatibility - will one kind of shop lead customers to use another? (eg, people may go out to buy a newspaper, then remember they need bread, milk, etc)

3) Will any shops be in competition w. yrs.?

4) Accessibility of the site

5) Suitability of the site itself - size, position, etc.

A large scale map or plan of the area would be useful. Visit the shopping centre at different times of the day & ∧days ∧different of the week and count the number of shoppers present.

It will be very difficult to make a forecast of potential sales, especially if you are thinking of starting up a completely new kind of business.

2

Introducing

Exercise 6

Open a document called Z6 and key in the following text using double line spacing and a ragged right-hand margin.

Note that **indented** paragraphs begin **five** spaces from the left-hand margin.

Save the document and print one copy.

ELEVENTH CENTURY FASHIONS *(centre e embolden heading)*

At the time of the Norman Conquest the style of dress worn universally was very simple. The standard lines of a tunic are shown in figure 1.

leave a space at least 2 inches (5 cm) by 2 inches for figure 1

Sleeves were tight-fitting, and several inches longer than the arm, and were pushed back in a series of folds. Tunics may have been split at the sides and finished with bands of embroidery, painstakingly sewn by the wearer's female relations. Other items of clothing were known as 'braies' and 'hose'. 'Braies' were simple trousers made of linen. They were bound at the lower leg either with cross gartering, or with the short hose from knee to ankle. The 'hose' usually had no foot, unless they were made of felt or leather when they were fashioned like a long boot. Usually shoes were worn on bare feet.

Women wore loose and rather shapeless draping garments. These consisted of a linen shift below a woollen robe cut rather like the men's tunics. The head was never uncovered (except in the case of very young girls). Headware might consist of a small veil covering head and shoulders, or a large scarf draped over the head, with the ends crossed under the chin and thrown back over the shoulders.

leave a space at least 2 inches (5 cm) by 2 inches for figure 2

Introducing

▶ HEADERS AND FOOTERS

Exercise 7

Recall document Z1 and make the following additions and alterations to the text. Change to a ragged right-hand margin. It will now take up more than one page, so **number** the pages in any suitable position.

Insert the header **ELTON RIDING CLUB**.

Insert the footer **CAMPBELL'S FARM, LOXTON GATE**.

Save the document and print one copy.

INFORMATION SHEET 10

JUMPING

leave
a space
2in × 2in
(5cm × 5cm)
for
logo

PREPARATION

For jumping, your stirrup leathers need to be 2 or 3 holes shorter than for hacking. The reason for this is that you have to raise your body out of the saddle while jumping and shorter leathers make it easier to do so.

As an introduction to jumping, walk the pony over a pole lying on the ground. Use a pole about 4 inches thick which the pony will be able to see without difficulty and which will not be broken if he treads on it.

Approaching the pole from either side, trot over it once or twice and then repeat the exercise at the canter. Now raise the pole about 6 inches and do the same thing.

CAVALLETTI

This is a good type of jump for the beginner. The poles are fixed to cross pieces at each end so that the height of the pole alters when the ends are rotated. Six inches from the ground is the lowest height, 18 inches the highest. ~~The cavalletti trains the horse to look where he is going, pick his feet up and approach obstacles calmly.~~

A line of cavalletti will ~~normally~~ usually consist of 6 or more poles all set at the same height and positioned in a straight line at about 4 foot intervals. A single jump can be made by placing one pole from the cavalletti on top of another, or by standing 2 poles side by side. The overall height should be about 18 inches and the width about 2 feet.

HOW TO JUMP

You can make a very simple jump by putting one pole from the cavalletti on top of another, or by placing 2 poles side by side.

The distance between the poles depends on yr. pony's stride.

As he lands, the pony's weight is taken on the forehand, so swing back slightly to redress the balance. Come back into the saddle w. a straight back, & look ∧ for what may lie ahead. ∧ out

To take off, trot towards the jump w. yr. seat ∧ raised slightly above the saddle, yr. weight resting on knees & feet. Keep your legs closed tight against the saddle. The pony will push himself into the air w. a thrust of the hindlegs. You shd. swing forward at this moment to go along w. the pony's movement. While in the air remain still but supple, ~~if~~ any ∧ movement ~~you move you~~ ∧ may cause the pony to lower his hindlegs & thus hit the jump.

WHAT HAPPENS IF...?

The Pony Refuses:

We call it a refusal when the pony (stops) suddenly at the jump. The angle ~~of~~ approach may have been wrong, or he may have lost interest (thro. boredom), or the jump may be too high. It is up to you to find out the cause of the refusal, if possible, & put right anything you can. It is a good idea to encourage the pony to make the jump afterwards, even if it means lowering it to the ground. Then give him a pat & take him away. NEVER lose your temper!

The Pony hits the jump:

There cd. be any number of reasons why this happens. Some may be the same as for refusing. Check whether your pony is unwell.

THE MAIN POINTS ARE:

(inset by one inch (2.5 cm))

1) Do not overjump
2) Do not make your pony jump when he is unwilling — find out what the matter is
3) Do not jump if the ground is hard
4) Do not jump if your pony is unwell
5) Use yr. legs and not your whip
6) KEEP YOUR TEMPER!

The pony Runs Out:

We call it 'running out' when a pony runs to the side of the jump, and avoids going over it. Many of the reasons will be the same as those mentioned above, but this is ~~a trick~~ also a wilful pony sometimes tries.

As a general rule, make sure your pony is fit & that he is getting plenty of exercise, but don't keep practising the same jumps as this will bore him — both you & yr. pony need variety.

Exercise 8

Open a document called Z8 and key in the following text and tables. Save the document and print one copy.

EXAMPLE ONE: Sandra - a part-time employee

Sandra has been in the firm's average pay scheme for 10 years. When she comes to retire, she will get a fixed amount of pension for each year her earnings were within a specified band. The bands and the number of years she was in each are:

Earnings band (annual)	amount of pension for each year	number of years earnings within band
up to £3,999	£50	2
£4,000 up to £5,999	£60	4
£6,000 and over	£75	4

Sandra's pension from this scheme will be
(2 x £50) + (4 x £60) + (4 x £75) = £640 a year

EXAMPLE TWO: George - a full-time employee

George's pensionable earnings at the time he retires are £24,000 a year. He has belonged to the firm's pension scheme for 30 years. The pension provided by the scheme is one-sixtieth of salary for each year of membership. George's pension works out to be

1/60 x 30 x £24,000 = £12,000 a year

(A scheme paying one-eightieth for each year and using the same definition of pensionable earnings would have produced a pension of £9,000 a year.)

Recall document Z8 and key in the following text, inserting the tables in the appropriate positions. Use double line spacing, but retain single line spacing for the tables. **Note** that all headings, paragraphs, and numbers in text should be standardised (numbers occurring in tables should remain as digits).

The revised document will now go into more than one page: insert the header **PENSIONS**, and number the pages at bottom centre.

Save the document and print one copy.

HOLD & BAGSHOTT INVESTMENT ADVISORS ← embolden

PENSIONS INFORMATION SHEET

Types of Pension

→ embolden

With a (money purchase scheme) the pension recd. depends on the amount of money paid in by you & how it has grown as a result of the scheme's investments by the time you retire. This fund is then used to buy you a pension.

embolden ←

With a (final pay scheme) the pension is worked out according to a formula and depends on yr. earnings near retirement and the number of yrs. you have belonged to the scheme. [There are some different, relatively rare, pension schemes.

embolden

With an (average pay scheme) the pension is based on your pay during each yr. you belonged to the scheme. The disadvantage of this scheme is that your pay during the early yrs. is likely to have been low, & this may drag down the average.

The employer contributes a percentage for each employee, and this is added to the employee's contribution & is allocated to the employee's 'fund'.

There are two main types of pension scheme: 'money purchase' and 'final pay'.

EXAMPLE ONE

How the Pension is Calculated

Theoretically, a money purchase scheme & a final pay scheme could provide a pension of exactly the same amounts for an individual, but the way the pensions are calculated is quite different.

embolden

With a (flat-rate) scheme you will get a fixed amount of pension for each yr. of membership. This kind of scheme has the same disadvantage as average pay schemes, & is made even worse by the fact that increases in earnings are totally ignored.

Final Pay Scheme

A pension worked out in this kind of scheme is linked to yr. earnings at the time you leave the scheme & yr. service with the employer. If you remain in the scheme until retirement, your pension will have kept pace w. increases in pay.

Yr. pension on retirement will depend on

single line spacing

I The number of years that count as pensionable, ie the length of time you have been a member of the scheme

II What you are earning at the time you retire

3 The proportion of earnings for each yr. in the scheme, usually based on sixtieths or eightieths.

EXAMPLE TWO

GLOSSARY

Blocks   strings of words, sentences or paragraphs.

Carriage return   the key (often simply called RETURN) that is used to mark the end of a line or paragraph.

Centring   placing a word or group of words, such as a heading, in the middle of the page or screen, between the two margins.

Creating a document   (or opening a document) the action of starting and naming a new piece of text which the word processor will treat as a complete unit.

Cursor   a small flashing square or line on the screen that indicates where changes in text should be made, or where text should be keyed in.

Cut and paste   a function of word processors that allows sections of text to be moved within a document.

Decimal tab   a special tab stop that can be used to line up columns of figures correctly at the decimal point.

Default   a setting (such as margins and line spacing) that has been pre-programmed in a word processing package remaining in force until altered by the operator.

Delete   a key that erases characters on the screen.

Disk drive   the device by which information and instructions are carried on to the disk, enabling documents to be stored.

Document   a piece of text recognised by the word processor as one complete unit.

Editing a document   making changes to a piece of text while it is on screen.

Floppy disk   a disk made of flexible plastic.

Font   style and size of characters.

Footers   information that is printed at the bottom of each page of a document.

Format   the layout for a piece of text.

Fully-blocked style   a very common style of layout in which all headings, paragraphs, etc, begin at the left-hand margin.

Hard disk   a disk made of rigid material.

Hardware   the parts of a word processor that can be handled (such as VDU, keyboard, printer, disks).

Headers   information which is printed at the top of each document.

Housekeeping   keeping the contents of a disk up-to-date by erasing unwanted documents.

Inset   changing the margins within a document so that the width of the text varies.

Justified   straight margin.

K   an abbreviation for kilobyte, which is a measurement of disk memory. It is 1024 characters (or bytes).

Line spacing   the number of lines measured vertically (down).

Merge   combining text from different documents.

Margin   the barriers to text at left and right of page or screen.

Mouse   a device held in the hand for moving a cursor on the screen.

Moving blocks   (another phrase for 'cut and paste') altering the position of a section of text within a document.

Network a number of computers linked together.

NLQ Near Letter Quality — a quality of print suitable for business correspondence.

Orphan line the last line of a paragraph appearing alone at the top of a page.

Page break a marker for the end of a page.

Pitch the size of characters (when printed). Usually word processors give 10 or 12 characters to the inch (2.5 cm.) measured horizontally (across), but often other sizes are available.

Qwerty the most widely used keyboard layout in the world, deriving its name from the first six letters on the top row.

Ragged right text that is unjustified, with a 'ragged' appearance at the right-hand margin. The left-hand margin will be straight.

Scrolling the way in which text can be viewed on screen, appearing to move like a scroll, with the top line disappearing as another line comes into view at the bottom.

Search and replace a function of word processors in which a word or phrase can be searched for and replaced by a new word or phrase.

Shared resource two or more word processors sharing an item of hardware, such as a printer.

Software programs that carry sets of instructions to the hardware.

Standardising making sure that there is no variation of layout styles within a document.

Tab stop a point where the cursor will stop when the tab key is pressed (helpful when keying in columns).

VDU Visual Display Unit, the name used for screen and keyboard.

Widow line the first line of a paragraph appearing alone at the bottom of a page.

Work station a place where someone can work having access to keyboard, screen and other resources.

Wraparound a function of word processors enabling the operator to carry on keying in without having to keep pressing the RETURN key, as line-endings are made automatically.

WYSIWYG What You See Is What You Get, text will be printed exactly as seen on screen.